100 DAYS OF Joy and Strength

CANDACE CAMERON BURE

100 Days of Joy and Strength
© 2025 Candace Cameron Bure

Published in Grand Rapids, Michigan, by Zondervan. Zondervan is a registered trademark of The Zondervan Corporation, L.L.C., a wholly owned subsidiary of HarperCollins Christian Publishing, Inc.

Requests for information should be addressed to customercare@harpercollins.com.

Unless otherwise noted, Scripture quotations are from the Holy Bible, New International Version®, NIV®. Copyright © 1973, 1978, 1984, 2011 by Biblica, Inc.® Used by permission of Zondervan. All rights reserved worldwide. www.zondervan.com. The "NIV" and "New International Version" are trademarks registered in the United States Patent and Trademark Office by Biblica, Inc.®

Any internet addresses (websites, blogs, etc.) and telephone numbers in this book are offered as a resource. They are not intended in any way to be or imply an endorsement by Zondervan, nor does Zondervan vouch for the content of these sites and numbers for the life of this book.

All rights reserved. No part of this publication may be reproduced, stored in a retrieval system, or transmitted in any form or by any means—electronic, mechanical, photocopy, recording, or any other—except for brief quotations in printed reviews, without the prior permission of the publisher.

Cover & interior design: Kathy Mitchell
Art direction: Tiffany Forester

ISBN 978-0-3104-6624-6
ISBN 978-0-3104-6799-1 (audiobook)
ISBN 978-0-3104-6798-4 (eBook)

Printed in Canada
25 26 27 28 29 FRI 10 9 8 7 6 5 4 3 2 1

INTRODUCTION

A governor of ancient Israel once encouraged his disheartened people with these words: "Do not grieve, for the joy of the LORD is your strength" (Nehemiah 8:10). Have you ever claimed those words as your own: "The joy of the Lord is my strength"?

On days when the Pacific breezes are cooling my patio and my work is humming along and the entire family is gathered around the dinner table, laughing, I easily relate to the joy part of that verse. It's very real to me.

But many times I've needed the strength of the Lord. When I went on live television each morning to cohost *The View*, when I've faced criticism on social media, and when I left acting to become a full-time mom—and then again, ten years later, as I prayerfully decided how and when to return to work.

The help of heaven has been constantly available in my day-to-day juggling act as a woman, a wife, a mom, a working mom, and most importantly, as someone who longs to point people to God in whatever I do or say. Yet as a doer and dreamer with lots of plans, I haven't always taken time to access those resources. The older I get, though, the easier it is for me to admit: I need all the joy and strength God will give me! Especially His joy and strength!

For the next one hundred days, let's take this journey as sisters, praying for each other and exploring the various ways the Lord can be both our joy and our strength. Whether we're having an ocean-breezy day, a lacking-courage day, a messy-house day, or an I'm-overwhelmed-and-can't-do-another-thing kinda day, God can remain the center and the focus of it all. And we and those we love will be better for it.

In this together,

Candace

WITH YOU IN MIND

DAY 1

God has a plan for how He'd like each of us to spend the next twenty-four hours. He has prepared this day ahead of time (literally), like a mom packing an amazing lunch for each member of her family, complete with energizing superfoods, a love note, and some of each person's favorite snacks. Yet if we aren't running our plans by Him first, we're prone to either jam-pack our schedules with junk or, at the very least, with things that may not be bad for us . . . but that aren't necessarily the best for us either.

Don't be discouraged—just be aware of it. Before you commit to today's "places to be" and "things to do," ask God what He has prepared for you. After all, He made the day with you in mind. You can trust what He has awaiting you.

PROVERBS 3:5–6 NKJV

Trust in the L̲o̲r̲d̲ with all your heart, and lean not on your own understanding; in all your ways acknowledge Him, and He shall direct your paths.

PRAYER

Thank You, Lord, that You take such great care of my daily life. Because You are trustworthy, I give You full access to my schedule today.

A HEALTHY DOSE OF GRATITUDE

DAY 2

Are you needing a boost of joy and strength for your day? Try adding a healthy dose of gratitude to your routine. Include a time of praise and worship as you exercise; post five things you're thankful for on social media, your bathroom mirror, or your household whiteboard; or share what you most appreciate from your day over dinner with someone you love. The method doesn't matter as much as establishing the habit—a habit of praise.

God's gifts don't need fancy packaging to qualify for gratitude. Most of life happens in the small surprises and simple pleasures. That means anything counts! From an extra-long hug from your child, to another driver letting you in front of them during a rough commute, to trying on a beautiful new shade of lipstick or enjoying a taste of chocolate after a good meal, God's goodness is all around. We just need to be watching for it.

A thankful heart can't help but mine deeper and deeper for the gems that are within each new day. Likewise, a grateful mind keeps looking higher and higher, above life's difficulties or frustrations, to the One who is above it all. Even on our worst days, we can thank God because we trust that He sees the bigger picture and He has good plans for us. There's really nothing like a healthy dose of gratitude. Don't do a day without it!

JAMES 1:17 NASB

Every good thing given and every perfect gift is from above, coming down from the Father of lights, with whom there is no variation or shifting shadow.

PRAYER

Lord, I choose to be mindful of the blessings You've built into my day. From the greatest miracle to what seems ordinary, I know these blessings come from You.

SECRET TO SUCCESS

DAY 3

I think I've found it—one of the Bible's secrets to success! From the leading men and women of Israel, to the Old Testament prophets serving as God's spokesmen, to the New Testament apostles on their missionary journeys, they were able to go out and do big things for God because they never went on assignment without Him.

God specifically appointed Moses to lead the Israelites out of Egypt and to the promised land. Though the Lord had made His choice crystal clear with a voice speaking from a burning bush, Moses was nevertheless feeling overwhelmed by the task ahead.

I hear his exasperation when he said (I'm paraphrasing Exodus 33:12–15): "Lord, You've been telling me, 'Lead these people on this mission.' You've assured me that You know me by name and I've found favor with You. Yet I still don't know who You're sending with me to help me. Unless it's You, we shouldn't be going at all."

God responded by pledging Himself to His servant: "I will be the One. I will go with you."

Are you needing to hear those words today as much as I am? We know upfront that not every undertaking from God will go without a hitch. Remember Israel's forty years in the desert? My version of that is the twenty years or so I've spent advocating as needed for more wholesome scripts with the writers and directors I work with. For every script change I do get, there may be three or four that stay in as written. Even so, every little difference gains more ground toward the goal. Every little difference honors and pleases God.

As you resume your divine assignment this day, press on in the presence and power of the Lord, taking to heart what God commanded Moses' successor, Joshua: "Be strong and courageous. Do not be afraid; do not be discouraged, for the LORD your God will be with you wherever you go" (Joshua 1:9). The Mighty Warrior of heaven knows you by name, and He will be at your side every step of the way. Don't leave home without Him!

ZEPHANIAH 3:16–17

On that day they will say to Jerusalem, "Do not fear, Zion; do not let your hands hang limp. The LORD your God is with you, the Mighty Warrior who saves."

PRAYER

You promise to go before me and behind me, Lord.
I'm counting on You. Stay right here with me.

BACK TO THE BASICS

DAY

As you're reading this, is someone in your life (other than God) trying to tell you who you should be or what you should be doing? Are you getting tripped up by what somebody else wants of you? Or maybe what they think of you?

Then go back to the basics. Take it to God in prayer first. Next, affirm who you are in His eyes. Restate your purpose—or define it if you haven't already. Clarify your priorities and values. Discuss them with people you trust. And use those foundational truths to set up boundaries: "These are my goals. This is who I am. Here are the nonnegotiables that I will not compromise."

When you have convictions and standards you want to uphold, it's easier to stand strong and say no. Not easy, but easier. Those basics are also the keys that open the doors to the dreams and plans God wants you going after.

1 JOHN 3:1 NLT

See how very much our Father loves us, for he calls us his children, and that is what we are! But the people who belong to this world don't recognize that we are God's children because they don't know him.

PRAYER

Sometimes I feel myself being drawn to perform based on what others think of me or need from me. Lord, direct my focus to being the person You know me to be, the person You created me to be.

WONDER WOMAN

DAY 5

Ah, Wonder Woman: strong, beautiful, bold, fearless, never gives up—an unconquerable warrior. She is by far my favorite superhero. I even have shoes and a coffee mug with her on them!

If you've ever read Proverbs 31, then you know the wonder woman described there is imposing, too, to say the least. She seems to have it all and do it all without missing a beat! She's remarkably successful in her work, respected in her community, adored by her family, cherished by her man, able to keep up with the sewing and laundry and bills—and apparently her house is spotless too.

Who wouldn't want to be her? At the same time, who could ever be her? Her life just isn't realistic.

That is, until we understand what often gets missed in reading the biblical description. Proverbs 31 isn't a capsule of a woman's calling at any one time; it shows every woman a standard across time, in the various seasons of her life. In other words, we can do it all, just not all at the same time.

What a difference that makes! God doesn't expect His daughters to be all things to all people at all times. He wants us to be faithful in the season we're in right now, obedient to the priorities He has for us at this time, witnesses wherever He has us.

No matter the season you're in, you have an opportunity to serve God in a way that you won't have again. So make the most of it. Show up and be present. Dedicate yourself to what's in front of you. That's what God's real wonder women do.

ECCLESIASTES 3:1 NCV

There is a time for everything, and everything on earth has its special season.

PRAYER

Lord, You know I've often tried to do it all at once, and it's only left me exhausted and discouraged. Thank You for creating seasons so I can be more present to today's joy and focused on the good gifts You're providing.

HOLY DAYS

DAY 6

In God's eyes, each day of our lives is a holy day, not just those times we're in church.

That word *holy* sounds so intimidating. But don't let it scare you. Holy simply means set apart or dedicated to God. Once He has your heart, you'll probably pretty naturally start committing other parts of your life to His service, including your home, your time, and your priorities. Still, our most prayerful commitments can be waylaid by those pesky, inevitable interruptions to our schedule. What then?

Some of them are actually "holy disruptions" sent by God to encourage and use and grow us in unexpected ways. Others are unwise distractions that draw our attention away from what He has destined for us. The Bible's timeless principles and the guiding voice of the Holy Spirit can help us discern the difference. So can the convictions and passions God has individually placed in our hearts.

It begins, though, with remembering that each day is gifted to us for serving God and others. Keeping this truth in mind will diminish the false urgency of the things that can actually wait for another day (or never!). It's also a sure way to multiply our peace, our joy, and our productivity throughout each day.

NEHEMIAH 8:10

This day is holy to our Lord.

PRAYER

God, supply me with the discernment to know which interruptions are invitations from You and which are nothing more than distractions. My heart is set on following Your invitation because it always leads me to something good!

LETTING GO

DAY 7

The world will tell you that the ultimate success is a big bank account, or being famous, or having a husband and kids. If we're honest, though, many of us define success by our ability to either juggle all the demands of life or control what happens in our worlds. But the real test of success is our friendship with God and the depths to which we trust Him.

I learned this firsthand. I'm a very motivated person and a really hard worker who gives 100 percent in whatever I do, so I'm used to ambitiously hunting down success. But there came a time in my life when I had to let go of trying to make success happen and start being available to what God had for me. That meant setting aside my desires to keep acting in order to stay at home and be the primary caretaker of our kids.

The cry of the surrendered heart is "Here I am, God. Use me however You choose." For people like me who prefer to be in control, reaching this place of surrender is as challenging as it sounds. But there is a big upside: Once you're there, it takes the pressure off success. You no longer have to be responsible for it. You can focus on being faithful, letting God handle the success of your efforts.

He will, you know. And you'll be able to be fully present to everything He is doing in you and through you.

GALATIANS 2:20 GW

I no longer live, but Christ lives in me. The life I now live I live by believing in God's Son, who loved me and took the punishment for my sins.

PRAYER

You are the One who can be trusted with the depths of my dreams and desires. As I surrender control, increase my trust that You'll work all things for what You know is best.

CIVIL DISCOURSE

DAY

It's been said that we are living in an "outrage culture," one divided by hostilities and tensions and divisions that you may feel powerless to change. But you are not powerless. Neither do you have to remain silent. Instead, be the person in your circle who is known for their civil discourse—conversation that is seasoned with kindness, gentleness, patience, and self-control.

God gives the fruit of His Spirit to everyone who has a relationship with Him, and those traits set the tone not only for our lives but for our speech. Kindness may not always win the argument, but it wins in a mightier way. And, it's classy. It is also one of the evidences that God is in you, even if you opt not to say a word.

There are times, though, when we need to speak up. Rather than joining in the outrage and beating people up verbally and emotionally, be ready with a gentle reply. And wait your turn. Listen humbly with respect and compassion. Listening leads to empathy. And with empathy comes a heartfelt response because out of the heart, the mouth speaks (see Luke 6:45).

You're never going to please or pacify everybody, but you can make sure you do right by people. And that includes your adversaries. In a world divided, multiply kindness.

You never know how loudly your actions might speak. Remember, kind *is* the new classy!

2 TIMOTHY 2:25-26 NLT

Gently instruct those who oppose the truth. Perhaps God will change those people's hearts, and they will learn the truth. Then they will come to their senses and escape from the devil's trap.

PRAYER

I prefer to represent You over my desire to be heard. God, make clear when I should speak and when to stay silent, and guide my choice of words to create a safe environment for You to change people's hearts.

THINK ON THESE THINGS

DAY 9

If forming good habits were easy, we'd all be happy, healthy, and fit comfortably in that cute party dress. But it's the good habits that give us a run for our money, right? Which means we need to bring our best to the effort.

If you're struggling to develop a new habit, it might help to ask yourself: "What's holding me back? Is it fear, a lack of motivation, or a lack of information about how to reach my goal?" A little research or a life coach can go a long way in providing the how-tos. And in scripture after scripture, God encourages us to "be strong and courageous" because the battles we face are actually His to win, if only we will seek His help. Bringing Him into the fight with us makes fear start to fall away.

As for motivation, why not try putting mindfulness to work for you? The Bible advises us: "Whatever is pure, whatever is lovely, whatever is admirable—if anything is excellent or praiseworthy—think about such things" (Philippians 4:8). After you've done something consistently, you know how good it feels and how beneficial it is for you. So the next time you're tempted to stay in bed instead of getting up to exercise, don't give power to your tiredness. Think instead on how much happier you'll be once you've finished your workout. Think on the good results you're achieving—better health, more confidence, a stronger body, a longer life with the people you love. And think on the fact that you're worth it. God says so. And if He says so, you can believe it! Then put your feet on the floor and keep pushing to be your best. The future you will thank you.

PHILIPPIANS 4:8 ESV

Whatever is true, whatever is honorable, whatever is just, whatever is pure, whatever is lovely, whatever is commendable, if there is any excellence, if there is anything worthy of praise, think about these things.

PRAYER

I stand in awe that You are more than willing and able to fight the hard battles with me. As I invite You into the process, dread and fear will diminish, and healing and renewal can begin.

TUNED IN

DAY 10

When life is going at full tilt, it's easy to lose sight of the "why" of what we're doing. And as soon as we lose our "why," the "who" we're trying to serve can become a little fuzzy as well. Thankfully, we can redeem the time and live it for all it's worth by tuning our spiritual dials to what matters.

It's important that we invest in the right things, not all things. For me, the right things come down to what deepens my relationship with God, what benefits my family, and what I'm called to. If my family and I make decisions based on these priorities, God always seems to take care of the rest. So when I'm deciding on a new business opportunity, for example, I discuss it with my husband and sometimes my kids—if it affects them too—and we explore, "Does this makes sense for us?" If it can't be kept in balance, if it will mess with our established priorities, then it needs to be a no. (Note: A challenging investment or a step of faith that may cause fear does not mean it falls into the safety net of a no.)

Over the years, I've said no a lot more often than I've said yes. Ultimately, my hope and trust in God keep me believing that for every no, there's something else around the corner that will be a better fit; I just need to hang in there and wait for the next opportunity. The same is true for you. You can trust that God is at work when He asks you to wait on Him for the next right thing.

EPHESIANS 5:16 GNT

Make good use of every opportunity you have, because these are evil days.

PRAYER

No one has better plans for every area of my life than You. I believe it with my mind; now write it on my heart as well. Your wisdom is my compass and my security.

IN HIS PRESENCE

DAY **11**

Like me, you've probably heard public officials or preachers, particularly at national holidays, quote the verse from 2 Corinthians 3 that says, "Where the Spirit of the Lord is, there is liberty" (v. 17 NKJV). The Bible also encourages us that we find more than freedom in God's presence; we also receive strength and joy (Psalm 16:11; Nehemiah 8:10).

I love that, don't you? I'll bet you can remember at least a few times when your spirits were instantly lifted at the sight of a family member or friend walking through the door to be with you. God similarly ministers to us, except that He is right there with us in every situation. On those days where we're feeling our weakest or the most hurried, He enters in, bringing us exactly what we need, just when we need it. Just in time.

1 CHRONICLES 16:27 HCSB

Splendor and majesty are before Him; strength and joy are in His place.

PRAYER

I'm moved by the way You show up and quietly strengthen me, turning my day around. Thank You for never leaving me to go through life alone.

CONTAGIOUS

DAY **12**

Have you ever noticed how contagious generosity is? When I see someone going out of their way to help somebody else, I'm inspired. It makes me want to do the same.

That ripple effect of kindness has to be God at work in our lives. It can't be just a coincidence that when the person ahead of you in the drive-through line offers to pay for your order, you suddenly want to pay for the car behind you. Scientists say that the boost of happiness we feel in that moment is a chemical reaction within our bodies.[1] Yes, sure. But I also believe it is God smiling on us with pleasure.

I'm guilty, though, of sometimes being so focused on my to-do list that I forget to be looking for ways to surprise people. Nevertheless, I want to get better at passing along the blessings. Maybe as we make acts of kindness contagious, others will join with us to pay it forward until no one is left untouched. Wouldn't that be something? May it start with you and me, starting today!

1 CHRONICLES 29:17 HCSB

I have willingly given all these things with an upright heart, and now I have seen Your people who are present here giving joyfully and willingly to You.

PRAYER

I bring You open hands and an open heart today, God. Open my eyes as well so that I don't miss that person You want me to bless.

MOVING TOWARD JOY

DAY 13

Have you ever moved into a new home? I have. Several times, actually. And the truth is: I haven't always celebrated those moves.

Sometimes they've been ultra-stressful; sometimes they've been sad, like when I left my family, friends, and work behind, not to mention LA's sunshine, to move to Montreal after Val and I were married. That one was really tough! (Not the being with Val part, but the cold weather, no friends, distant-city part.) Thankfully, God has taught me that, no matter where in the world I am—a tiny trailer on a movie set, a snowbound rental apartment in the frozen tundra, or a house hugged by sunshine—I can always dedicate that dwelling, temporary or permanent as it may be, to God.

That's what our family did when we renovated our current home. After we tore it down to the studs, each of us not only wrote our names and Scripture verses on the structural "bones" of our home, but we gathered in the eventual living room to pray over the house and ask God's blessing on each person who would ever come through its doors.

When we dedicate our spaces to God's glory (work and hobby spaces too!), He knows just how to help us make them places of warmth and joy and community, where others feel welcomed and He is celebrated.

EZRA 6:16 HCSB

Then the Israelites, including the priests, the Levites, and the rest of the exiles, celebrated the dedication of the house of God with joy.

PRAYER

God, I invite You and others into my home, wherever "home" is. Guide me to dedicate this place to You and celebrate Your presence here with joy.

REPEATING HISTORY

DAY **14**

Moses' successor, Joshua, made the declaration in today's verse at a time in history when his people, Israel, were extremely vulnerable to the influence of other cultures and religions. Seeing the world our kids are growing up in, I can't help but feel that we're living in a similar age. It's as if history is repeating itself, and frankly, it's a little scary. Parenting has always had its challenges—every generation's moms and dads have tried to safely guide their children through not just homework and makeup but dating and friendships. Now, though, we have to add social media and the internet to that mix.

Obviously, as parents (or as people who care about the well-being of the children in our lives), we can't protect the younger generation from every harmful influence, but we can set good boundaries. We can uphold rules and expectations that will help them live more innocently. We can encourage the positive use of their giftings. And we can affirm again and again not only whom we serve but what we stand for.

It will be a daily choice for them, just as it is for us. Yet if we regularly uphold God's place in our lives, we just might see history repeat itself once again, but in the best of ways: where our kids and grandkids choose to serve the same God as their fathers (and mothers!). That feels like a legacy worth striving for!

JOSHUA 24:15 ESV

Choose this day whom you will serve, whether the gods your fathers served . . . or the gods of the Amorites in whose land you dwell. But as for me and my house, we will serve the LORD.

PRAYER

I choose You today, God, and I pray that You will move in the same way in the hearts of the kids I know and love. Lead us all in the way we should go.

TITLED AND TRUE

DAY **15**

I remember all the years when I identified with faith, but only as a title. I called myself a "Christian," yet Christ didn't really factor into my decisions or my actions.

As with any title, though—wife, mother, daughter, sister, or whatever position you might hold at work—there comes a time when you find out if what you claim is for real or if it's just words. I think the proof comes when you're willing to sacrifice to stay true. A devoted mom will give up sleep in the middle of the night to hold her little girl when that child is sick. A faithful sister will step in to watch her nieces or nephews when their parents have to be gone. A considerate boss will stay extra hours to help her team hit its deadline rather than leaving them to do all the work. In my own life, I knew I had genuinely committed my life to God when I turned down acting roles that didn't fit the convictions and priorities He had instilled in my heart.

Sacrifices like these can be inconvenient at best—and sometimes downright painful. But there is a certain deep-down joy in sacrifice, too, isn't there? As soon as we begin to line up our actions and choices with who we really are, it shows. Even while things are difficult, we radiate a peace and contentment that are not of this world. In a word, we start to shine. And so does the One whose name we claim.

PHILIPPIANS 2:14-15 ESV

Do all things without grumbling or disputing, that you may be blameless and innocent, children of God without blemish in the midst of a crooked and twisted generation, among whom you shine as lights in the world.

PRAYER

Jesus, I want to live true to all that You've called me to in this day. In every role of mine, align my will and my ways with Yours so that You shine through me.

ATTITUDE CHANGE

DAY **16**

Can you recall a time when you saw God actually change the mind of someone in authority—a boss or a professor, maybe, or your parents when you were young? You saw God change their minds so much that, rather than hindering something He had called you to, they supported what God is calling you to do? Me too. Those are such great surprises!

But then there are other times when it seems like everywhere we turn, we're facing a brick wall, right? While we wait for God to either intervene or redirect our efforts, it can be tempting to let impatience get the best of us. At least it is for me. Yet God asks us to keep trusting Him with an expectant heart (Psalm 5:3).

Not every day will be a "fully expectant and trusting Him" day; still, let's try. Let's ask Him to help us look to Him with a measure of hope and faith for the next twenty-four hours. Who knows? Maybe this will be the day that someone in charge decides to remove the obstacles that are standing in our way!

EZRA 6:22

For seven days they celebrated . . . because the L<small>ORD</small> had filled them with joy by changing the attitude of the king of Assyria so that he assisted them in the work on the house of God, the God of Israel.

PRAYER

Even if You don't change the attitude of that "king" in my life today, Lord, will You please keep a watch on my mind and spirit? I look to You with hope and anticipation, knowing You will somehow make a way for Your work to be done, whenever the time is right. And in the meantime, grant me Your patience.

A BIBLE BASH

DAY 17

When I read verses like Nehemiah 8:12—"All the people went away to eat and drink, to send portions of food and to celebrate with great joy, because they now understood the words that had been made known to them"—I'm always relieved that it's not just me; even the people in ancient times liked to celebrate with a party! But have I ever thrown a bash because the words of God suddenly made sense to me? No.

Maybe I should though. After all, it's a pretty big deal when words we've read over and over finally take root and bear fruit. We see it happen as our kids or mentees grow up and integrate the things we've been trying to instill in them for years (a cause for celebration if ever there was one!). I assume God feels a little like that, too, once we "get it," tucking away His words in our hearts.

As we dig into Scripture today, let's see what surprises He may have in store. And if something cool becomes clear for the first time, I promise to celebrate! Will you join me?

PHILIPPIANS 4:4

Rejoice in the Lord always. I will say it again: Rejoice!

PRAYER

Holy Spirit, I come to Your Word today, excited for what You may reveal to me and ready to celebrate it!

SHELTERED

DAY 18

If you've ever seen how a mother bird protects her eggs in a nest or the way a chivalrous man holds his coat over a woman during a rainstorm, then you have two pretty good pictures of our heavenly Father's care for us. Today, we are looking at Psalm 5:11: "Let all who take refuge in you be glad; let them ever sing for joy. Spread your protection over them, that those who love your name may rejoice in you." What I find most compelling about this verse is our part in it. The psalmist spoke of those who actively seek refuge in God.

I don't know about you, but I still have plenty to learn about seeking out God's protection instead of trying to withstand trouble on my own. For all the times my independent streak has proven to be a blessing, it also has its downsides.

Thankfully, God is patient and kind. He knows where we're weak and when we're most likely to act like children instead of the adults we are. Yet He keeps calling to us: "Here! I'm right here! Run to Me! I've got you!" That His protection is always available makes me feel loved and valued and safe. How blessed we are to be so tenderly loved and protected by Him!

PSALM 5:11

Let all who take refuge in you be glad; let them ever sing for joy. Spread your protection over them, that those who love your name may rejoice in you.

PRAYER

With You as my refuge, heavenly Father, I find both safety and strength. I praise You for loving me as You do.

WALK THIS WAY

DAY 19

More often than I can count, I've taken my own path rather than asking the Lord to show me His. And you know what? It's meant having to take the long way back to where I belong, time and time again.

Those detours and delays that I cause myself are so frustrating! In my day-to-day life—chores, errands, work—I like efficiency. I like taking the shortest distance from point A to point B. So why I sometimes veer from that spiritually is puzzling. It also makes me that much more thankful for the clear directions God does provide through His Word and the guiding presence of His Holy Spirit.

God gives us the freedom to choose whose route we will follow: His or ours. And although I still stubbornly plot my own course at times, if I think about it, I absolutely prefer a traveling Companion who simultaneously knows the way. So next time I come to a crossroads, will you do me a favor? Remind me to stop and ask God which way He's going and then walk it with Him. I'll try to do the same for you, so we can all skip those self-imposed detours and stay on the path that leads to life.

PSALM 16:11

You make known to me the path of life; you will fill me with joy in your presence, with eternal pleasures at your right hand.

PRAYER

God, remind me to listen for Your voice before I head down some unknown road. Teach me to heed Your directions instead of going my own way.

MAKEOVER

DAY **20**

The lovely Audrey Hepburn often quoted from a poem by an American humorist named Sam Levenson: "The beauty of a woman must be seen from in her eyes, because that is the doorway to her heart, the place where love resides."[2] It sure seems to be true that our eyes mirror our souls. When we're happy, people can see it. Instantly. When we're sad, that's apparent too. And when we're burdened by guilt or shame or fear, the weight shows in the windows of our souls first. We may try and mask it, but those who know us well can tell.

Once Jesus, the Light of the World, takes up residence in our hearts, the difference is just as obvious. You could say we start to sparkle within. His presence lights us up from the inside out, showing through in our attitudes and actions and words. And I don't mean just on the easygoing days, but in the rough-and-tumble times that really test our faith. What's more, our spiritual eyes open up, newly enlightened to the wisdom of God's counsel. Soon, His commands and instructions, which may have once felt like spiritual obligations we had to fulfill to stay in His graces, become open doors to a deeper trust in Him. Duty gives way to friendship because we love Him and can see that His ways are good.

Admittedly, this is a new idea for me. I haven't always thought of obedience as the means to a divine makeover, but what else would you call something that accentuates our eyes and makes us radiant? God is indeed in the beauty business, making each of us beautiful from the inside out.

PSALM 19:8

The precepts of the LORD are right, giving joy to the heart. The commands of the LORD are radiant, giving light to the eyes.

PRAYER

Nothing is like Your light in my life. Jesus, I pray for more of You as I read Your Word and represent You before others. May they see Your beauty in me.

YOUR SWEET SPOT

DAY **21**

My daughter, Natasha, was always one to retreat to her closet when she wanted to be alone. Often, I do the same thing myself. So it's refreshing that Jesus recommended going off somewhere by ourselves for some personal time with God (Matthew 6:6).

Your private getaway doesn't have to be a literal closet, although that absolutely works. I know of women who retreat to their laundry room, their car, their front porch or back deck, or a local park or walking trail. Because she had so many children running around, the mother of the great preachers Charles and John Wesley used to sit in a chair in the middle of her kitchen with her apron over her head for her prayer time.[3] (We mamas do what we have to!)

It makes no difference how or where you retreat; any solitary place can become your inner room. Just find that sweet spot and, from that personal "sanctuary," be you. Cry out to, consult with, journal to, or worship and praise the One who knows you best. God will meet us where we are.

MATTHEW 6:5–6 NASB

When you pray, you are not to be like the hypocrites; for they love to stand and pray in the synagogues and on the street corners so that they will be seen by people. . . . But as for you, when you pray, go into your inner room, close your door, and pray to your Father who is in secret; and your Father who sees what is done in secret will reward you.

PRAYER

Welcome to my prayer closet today, dear Lord. As I pour out my heart for Your ears only, please speak to me. I'm listening.

SEASON SONGS

DAY 22

Though I can carry a tune and I absolutely love to sing, I'm not a great singer. Then again, nobody ever said that fun has to have talent. (Can I get an amen?) I could be cleaning the house, running errands in the car, or getting ready for a date with my husband. Doesn't matter. If the right tune comes on, nothing can stop me from belting it out and rejoicing in the moment. Not even the embarrassment of my kids.

Of course, when Natasha, Lev, and Maks were babies, I sang them soothing little lullabies while rocking them to sleep. Lullabies that expressed my love for them and how safe they were in my arms. We parents seem to naturally do that. Apparently God our Father does it all the time as well; He sings His love over us. Which makes me wonder if His song choices vary depending on the season we're in? If maybe God holds each of us close and sings soothing words over us when we need comfort, but then, in times of celebration, He turns up the volume and rejoices over us with pride, and maybe dancing too?

I wouldn't put it past Him. The Lord of dance and the Composer of song loves us so much that He probably can't help but sing at the thought of us.

ZEPHANIAH 3:17 NKJV

The LORD your God . . . will rejoice over you with gladness, He will quiet you with His love, He will rejoice over you with singing.

PRAYER

I'm grateful for the ways You soothe me, Father God, and for Your delight in me. Your love makes me feel like singing.

HANG IN THERE

DAY **23**

You know that saying, "No good deed goes unpunished"? I don't know its origins, but somewhere along the way, somebody evidently got burned by someone they tried to help. Seeing that the apostle Paul urged the Christians in Galatia to "not grow weary while doing good" suggests that a lot of well-meaning believers were pretty discouraged (Galatians 6:9 NKJV). We don't know if they'd been burned by their own relatives, by strangers, or by other church members. Apparently, though, their attempts at doing good had been met with opposition, if not outright rejection.

Ugh. We've all been there. Unfortunately, some people really don't want to be helped. And it hurts. Paul knew how tiring it can be to keep putting ourselves out there. It's even possible that he was, in part, writing to himself, not just to the Galatians.

Sowing seeds of any kind is tough, time-consuming work. Sowing seeds of kindness has its own unique challenges because the human heart is as unpredictable as the weather! On the extra-tiresome days, it may be all we can do to hold on to God's promise of a harvest. Even so, hang in there and don't lose heart, friend. In due season, we shall reap the good that we have sown.

GALATIANS 6:9 NKJV

Let us not grow weary while doing good, for in due season we shall reap if we do not lose heart.

PRAYER

Be the lifter of my head, Lord. Refresh my spirit so I can go back out there and keep serving others. Please. I'm tired today.

THE CUTTING EDGE

DAY 24

If you've ever used a blunt knife to prepare a meal or tested out dull shears in your landscaping, you've experienced futility. It only takes a few coarse cuts to realize that an unsharpened edge requires a lot more effort to get the job done.

Attempting important tasks or big decisions while relying on our own know-how has the same effect: We work harder, not smarter . . . and still may not see a good result. The wisdom of God, present in both His Word and the counsel of His Spirit, is what makes us sharp, decisive, discerning—all those things we need to accomplish the goals God has given us.

King Solomon, writing from his breadth of experience, also informed us that God's wisdom is more powerful than physical strength or weapons of war (Ecclesiastes 9:16, 18). That's so amazing to me! On one hand, wisdom is useful for cutting through all the surface stuff and getting right to the core, saving us time, energy, stress, and heartache. That alone would be enough for me to want more of it. But to learn that it's also mightier than the things we typically equate with strength puts fresh wind in my sails.

Best of all, we never have to be without it. James 1:5 says that if any of us is ever lacking wisdom, all we have to do is ask God for it, and He will deliver. I assume I speak for all of us when I say, "Sign me up for that! I'm in!"

ECCLESIASTES 10:10 ESV

If the iron is blunt, and one does not sharpen the edge, he must use more strength, but wisdom helps one to succeed.

PRAYER

I'm asking for Your wisdom, God—more and more and more of it. I need it; I want it; I'm reliant on it. Help me, I pray!

FOR THE JOY

DAY 25

When was the last time you had "one of those days," where you had to force yourself to get out of bed to do what you needed to? What's that you say? Just this morning? (Smile, I'm just giving you a hard time.)

Jesus understands this for sure. While pouring His heart out to His Father in heaven prior to the events that would bring Him to the cross, He admitted that He didn't want to die in this way if there was any alternative. That's so understandable! Medical doctors and historians alike agree that crucifixion is as cruel and torturous a means of death as any that man has ever devised.

Still, Jesus endured it. There was no other way for His mission on earth to be accomplished. He was the only one qualified to be the substitute for our sins.

Jesus went through all the pain, disciplining his mind and will, says Hebrews 12:2, "because of the joy awaiting him" (NLT). If you think of a woman's commitment to endure hours of labor for the sake of holding her baby in her arms, you have some idea of Jesus' heart toward us, though on an eternal scale. He knew that His momentary suffering would achieve results that would make the sacrifice utterly worth it.

It's not an intuitive thought, but there actually is joy in obedience. That's what we forget when we're on the front end of lethargy or temptation. Yes, the taming of our will is hard. To die to self is as challenging as it gets. Obedience empties us of ourselves and tests our commitment. But in return, we grow stronger, gaining endurance and a surer sense of God's will. God becomes an increasingly greater force in our lives. And we are rewarded with joy beyond our circumstances now and a wondrous future with God, where there will be no more tears ever again.

---

2 CORINTHIANS 4:16-18

We do not lose heart. Though outwardly we are wasting away, yet inwardly we are being renewed day by day. For our light and momentary troubles are achieving for us an eternal glory that far outweighs them all. So we fix our eyes not on what is seen, but on what is unseen, since what is seen is temporary, but what is unseen is eternal.

PRAYER

I'll shift my focus off my circumstances and onto You today. I trust You when You say there is joy on the other side!

BUILT UP

DAY 26

Have you ever heard anyone say that maintaining a good marriage is harder than maintaining a good career? Chances are, many of us would agree with that. For two completely different, and very flawed, human beings to become a united front with a strong foundation isn't a short-term DIY project; it's an ongoing construction effort!

The ways to build up your marriage are as varied as the paint colors and finishes in a home-improvement store. Learning your spouse's love language and doing the little things to speak it have been real go-tos for Val and me throughout our marriage. Setting up a monthly date night or weekly lunch is a godsend for many couples, as is taking regular walks or exploring new adventures together.

You don't need grandiose efforts. Building the relationship brick by brick and day by day shores up the house just as surely as an extreme makeover. Without a doubt, though, you want to construct it on solid rock. God is vested in establishing strong marriages, and He will come alongside you and your spouse as a partner to accomplish just that.

If you're single or dating, these words are for you, too, as now is a prime time to build toward a great marriage by investing in your growth. The better the person you bring into your marriage, the better the two of you will be together. So dig in to good books, join a small group that will encourage you spiritually, seek out a mentor or life coach, and consider meeting regularly with a pastor or professional counselor for accountability and wisdom. I promise, you won't regret it.

JUDE 20–21

You, dear friends, by building yourselves up in your most holy faith and praying in the Holy Spirit, keep yourselves in God's love as you wait for the mercy of our Lord Jesus Christ to bring you to eternal life.

PRAYER

I don't want to do marriage without You.
You are my—and our—Rock. We need
You, Lord, now and always.

FOREVER PURSE

DAY **27**

Wouldn't it be wonderful if some designer invented a purse that never wears out, can't be stolen, and can't be ruined? On second thought, God has made it a possibility already—with the purse we carry around inside us in our heart of hearts.

Any great purse reserves space for our valuables—car keys, cell phone, wallet—along with our everyday essentials. You know, that favorite lipstick or mascara, sunscreen or moisturizer, a travel-size fragrance, and the requisite breath mints and hand sanitizer. After a few months of lugging around all that stuff, noticing my purse is getting heavier by the day, I'll dump it out and go through its contents to reorganize and get rid of the junk.

Our forever purse can use an occasional purging as well, because not everything that is taking up space in our hearts deserves to stay. Love does. The Word of God does. Friendship and family do. Faith, hope, peace, and service are some of our everyday essentials. Most other things we can leave out.

What are you collecting in your purse, and why? What treasures are you storing up, and for whom? Are you using them to ease the burdens of others? Are your everyday essentials, above all, enriching your love for God and people?

The purses of this life, as we women know all too well, grow old and useless if they don't go out of style first. The things of this earth are gone in an instant. Riches scatter like dandelion seeds in the wind. Jobs and houses, we leave behind. But a purse filled with the treasures of heaven is ever new.

LUKE 12:32-33

Do not be afraid, little flock, for your Father has been pleased to give you the kingdom. Sell your possessions and give to the poor. Provide purses for yourselves that will not wear out, a treasure in heaven that will never fail, where no thief comes near and no moth destroys.

PRAYER

Too many times I've stored up things that fade over time. Purge my daily goals and long-term priorities of any junk, and set my heart on eternity's riches—those blessings only You can give that never grow old or useless.

RIGHT WHERE YOU BELONG

DAY 28

Would you classify yourself as a participant or a spectator? Maybe because I've been working since I was in kindergarten, I'm inclined to get in there and get involved, regardless of what's going on.

Some people naturally seem to gravitate toward the action—if it's game on, they're a go. But others are completely the opposite—these friends tend to be slower to join in. But once they do enter the game, they make an incredible contribution.

The type of hesitancy to avoid is that which originates in something other than temperament. Our friends who are retired or ailing probably know it best, though stay-at-home moms can easily struggle with it too: the hesitancy brought about by buying in to our circumstances. Do you know what I mean? It's when you feel discarded, useless, relegated to the sidelines, and you suspect that's right where you belong.

It doesn't take much to think our best days are behind us. Well, think again, sisters. God has powerful work for you to do. You may no longer be part of the economic workforce, but you remain in the kingdom's workforce.

Your back may be bad, but if your mouth still works, you can tell your neighbor and your grandkids and your favorite waitress at the local restaurant about what a faithful friend Jesus is. You may be confined to a bed, but as long as you have breath and a heartbeat, you can be praying for everyone you know.

Life may have you on the sidelines, but you're still on the team. If you're on the team, you're still part of the game. If you're part of the game, you have a role to play. Get in there and give it your all. I'll be cheering you on.

COLOSSIANS 3:22–24 MSG

Do your best. Work from the heart for your real Master, for God, confident that you'll get paid in full when you come into your inheritance. Keep in mind always that the ultimate Master you're serving is Christ.

PRAYER

Lord, whether it's a day where I'm leading the charge or a day where I'm in the background, may I make every moment count. Thank You for picking me for Your team in the biggest game of all!

WALK THE TALK

DAY 29

Who needs integrity? We all do! Society trumpets the necessity of integrity for public figures such as politicians and CEOs, since people are reliant on them for their well-being or livelihood. But we're not exempt. People are also relying on us to be the same person in public and in private.

Happily, God has designed it so that with the responsibility comes great reward. Besides bringing us the kind of joy that comes only with peace of mind, being the same person at all times builds trust with others, creating space for our voice in their lives. That could be why, in Titus 2, Paul didn't launch into theology after calling Pastor Titus to sound teaching; the wise mentor discussed character, naming some of the defining traits of godly men and women of various ages (vv. 1–10).

I love that. Character communicates big-time, winning us an audience that we might never attract otherwise.

Until people see our words translating into our day-to-day lives, they won't care what we teach. The real impact is in walking the walk.

Representing Christ at His best means revealing Him in our walk and our talk. The walk takes precedence, at least with those who don't know Him. Jesus said, "Everyone who hears these words of mine and *puts them into practice* is like a wise man who built his house on the rock" (Matthew 7:24, emphasis mine). In essence, friends, if we're walkin' it, we're rockin' it.

PSALM 119:1-3 NLT

Joyful are people of integrity, who follow the instructions of the LORD. Joyful are those who obey his laws and search for him with all their hearts. They do not compromise with evil, and they walk only in his paths.

PRAYER

God, bring together my walk and my talk into one beautiful whole, even as You continue to develop my character.

CLASS ACTS

DAY **30**

Plays well with others. Remember that grade-card category from elementary school? My parents always emphasized the importance of sharing, politeness, and consideration to me and my siblings, and it's something that Val and I have placed a high value on with our own kids.

Others may choose to be mean, call people names, or spread rumors. Some people like to stir up drama or start fights. Let's not play that way. It diminishes us all as humans made in the image of God, and it diminishes people's opinion of our Dad in heaven.

We already know that our Dad is bigger than theirs and that our older Brother, Jesus, could take on anybody and win. So the fact that they both exhort us to take the high road means something.

The way our heavenly family operates is different from other families. Instead of "Fight back," we're taught to pray for the people who are taunting us. Instead of "Get revenge," we're advised to concentrate on doing what's right and leave the rest in wiser hands. Instead of "Eye for eye and tooth for tooth," we're told to keep our mouths closed and not lash out.

That kind of self-control is hard work at any age! The Holy Spirit, however—true Friend that He is—backs us up with extra support, encouraging us to stick by our convictions and not play to a lower level.

Our playmates may choose to throw dirt or pull hair, but we don't have to. We can be class acts, setting an example worth following that makes our Father proud.

HEBREWS 13:15-16

Through Jesus, therefore, let us continually offer to God a sacrifice of praise—the fruit of lips that openly profess his name. And do not forget to do good and to share with others, for with such sacrifices God is pleased.

PRAYER

Thanks for teaching me well and encouraging the high road. Bring those heavenly family values to mind whenever I need them today.

ANSWERED!

DAY 31

I suppose that anyone who prays has done this, but I've sometimes caught myself thanking God for "answered prayer," when what I really meant was "Thank You, God, for answering the way I wanted"! What I see in Scripture, though, is that whenever His sons or daughters pray, God answers; it's just that sometimes it's "No" or "Not now" or "This instead" rather than "Sure, here you go, child."

This has pushed me to examine myself and my reasons for praying in the first place. And it's been pretty convicting for me, to say the least. Is God solely my divine 911—my emergency standby—or my Friend whom I take everything to? Am I coming to Him only for His gifts or to know Him better? Do I pray as a spiritual-sounding means of getting what I want or to truly seek what God wants? And when He does answer, do I trust that He has me covered, no matter the answer?

The difference in my attitude matters more than I want to admit sometimes. And the litmus test is this: I'm deeply, actually relating to Him when I not only desire His will above my own, but when I can respond "I trust You, Lord" to any answer of His.

PSALM 17:6 TLB

Why am I praying like this? Because I know you will answer me, O God! Yes, listen as I pray.

PRAYER

I repent of being shortsighted in my relationship with You. Draw me deeper and deeper into our friendship, teaching me to seek You and Your will above all.

PLOT TWIST

DAY **32**

Just about everybody loves a good plot twist. It's the stuff that keeps us going to movies and buying novels and binge-watching our favorite series on Netflix. A good plot twist means a good story. And story is the stuff that legends are made of.

Plot twists are also the stuff that life is made of. Literally anything can change our story, from tragic circumstances such as an illness or an unexpected loss, to our choices, to another person's decision, to a job promotion, to an encounter with God, to an outright miracle.

The Bible is full of amazing plot twists like these. Abraham and Sarah having a baby in their old age, twenty-five years after that child was promised. Daniel being thrown in a den of lions and pulled out the next morning without a scratch on him. A virgin giving birth to the Son of God. Blind men receiving sight. And perhaps the greatest plot twist of all: a sinless Jesus betrayed by one of His closest friends, delivered to death on a cross, and resurrected three days later to defeat death once and for all.

Whatever plot twists you have been through—or possibly are enduring now—just know that in the drama, something divine is happening. Our Enemy, the devil, may be working overtime in hopes of turning our stories into tragedies, but God never sleeps. He has written our beginning and our end, and our storyline is never out of His trustworthy hands.

PSALM 121:3-4 NKJV

He who keeps you will not slumber. Behold, He who keeps Israel shall neither slumber nor sleep.

PRAYER

Right now I'm struggling with how my story is unfolding. I can't see where You're taking me, God. Help me to trust You despite my fear of what I can't control.

ONLY HUMAN

DAY 33

It seems like every woman I know—myself included—fears in her weakest moments that she isn't enough. That she's failing any number of people on a given day: her kids, her husband, her boss, her mother or mother-in-law, her friends . . . or, worst of all, God.

On those days, I keep coming back to the knowledge that God doesn't view me as a failure; He views me as human. That's such a relief to my spirit! His intimate awareness of how weak I am means that His expectations are realistic. He's not deluded about me; He's not fazed by my faults or surprised by my inadequacies. With each of us, He is clear on what we're capable of, what is impossible for us, and what we need from Him.

And He would know! He made us from dust, designing us with physical and intellectual boundaries from the very start. Once sin entered the picture, our limits multiplied. We became even more embedded in our humanity. More dependent.

It's as if we ended up on crutches. Still, God's response has never been, "What klutzes! Let them help themselves! They don't deserve My help." No, He hurries to our side to offer His strength and support, making up for what we lack. God even went as far as sending Jesus to bridge the gap between us so we can be in relationship with Him!

Let's grab His arm and lean in to Him today. Our God is strong where we are weak. Abundant where we are inadequate. And His love for us never, ever fails.

2 CORINTHIANS 12:9 THE VOICE

He said to me, "My grace is enough to cover and sustain you. My power is made perfect in weakness."

PRAYER

Where would I be, Father God, if You didn't know me so well? Thank You for Your love, which so readily soothes my sense of failure, and for Your grace, which sustains me in my weaknesses.

THE (WO)MAN IN THE MIRROR

DAY **34**

So many of us are doers by nature that when James challenged us to prove that we are doers of God's Word, you're probably thinking what I'm thinking: *Already am! Check. What's next?* Sometimes, though, it's little verses like this one that pack the biggest surprise, so I hope you don't mind, but I'd like to take a few minutes to look at what's here, just in case. Especially since the verses that follow James 1:22 offer an example of a mere hearer.

We're told of a guy who walks by a mirror, stops to glance at himself long enough to verify, "Yep, that's me all right!"—and then forgets what he looks like as soon as he walks away. Because I spend a lot of time in front of a mirror with my job, I wasn't sure what to make of this—I mean, how could he forget his own face?—until one Bible commentator put the illustration in perspective: "Thus is it often with the mirror of the soul."[4]

Ahhh, okay. We may recognize ourselves in a sermon or the life of a biblical figure enough to claim, "Yep, that's me!" in the moment, but once church is over or we've turned the page, it's "out of sight, out of mind." This quickly fading "knowledge" is very different from the deep awareness that arises from daily walks and talks with God. He reflects who we really are. And when we catch sight of ourselves in His mirror, it sometimes produces a penetrating, godly sorrow. A kind of good grief that compels us to reverse course because we've seen our sin and how it's hurting the One who loves us most.

I'm sad to say, I have been that (wo)man in the mirror, aware of

God's teachings but ignoring them; fleetingly telling God I'm sorry and then continuing to do what I wanted. Praise God for His forgiveness and for fresh starts once we finally see and repent!

To be a true doer of the Word means to act on the full knowledge of what we've read and heard. Anything less, said James, and we're only deceiving ourselves.

JAMES 1:22 NASB

Prove yourselves doers of the word, and not just hearers who deceive themselves.

PRAYER

Dear Father, I repent of the times I've heard Your truth but tossed it aside. Sensitize me to what breaks Your heart. Show me my face so I can be right with You.

AWAKENINGS

DAY 35

Have you ever wondered what it's like to be a newborn baby? Yes, I know we were all one of those once, but I mean, what if we could be inside the brain of a newborn and watch the fireworks?

Everything in an infant's world is a first. Scientists have reported that by the time a baby is three years old, his or her brain, which had one hundred billion neurons at birth, has increased to some one hundred trillion neural connections.[5] All those colors, sounds, faces, smells, tastes, and words must feel like miniature awakenings, bursting at the speed of microwave popcorn.

The Holy Spirit makes baby Christians just as capable of being awakened to all that a life in Christ entails. We're supernaturally equipped to grow by leaps and bounds from the moment of new birth. And with nurturing, we will.

God's Word offers a lifetime supply of both milk and meat, ensuring that we're nourished at every stage of development. Also, He has appointed the community of faith to come alongside us in discipleship and friendship and the Holy Spirit to spur on and complete what has started.

If you're new to this thing called faith, be sure to feed on God's Word every day and get connected with a mature group of Christians who will not only encourage your growth but help it along. Both of those things have made a huge difference for me.

Jesus said, "The words I have spoken to you—they are full of the Spirit and life" (John 6:63). Peter the apostle assured us that we've been given everything we need for life and godliness.

We have all of this so that we might not only grow, but grow up good and strong!

2 PETER 1:3-4

His divine power has given us everything we need for a godly life through our knowledge of him who called us by his own glory and goodness. Through these he has given us his very great and precious promises, so that through them you may participate in the divine nature.

PRAYER

Holy Spirit, keep me growing, and growing strong,
so that once I'm grown up, I will resemble You.

MAKE THEM COUNT

DAY **36**

Researchers have conservatively estimated that the average person speaks at least seven thousand words a day.[6]

My oh my, that's a lot of words coming at us, and a lot of words going out at other people!

"Think about what that means to you," remarks Paul Petrone, a senior editor at LinkedIn. "Those seven thousand words (at least) . . . are your imprint on the world. They dictate how people perceive you—and largely define you."[7]

Our words also deeply influence how the world perceives the God we serve. Are we making them count or letting them go out empty?

Throughout the book of Proverbs, the wisest human being who ever lived commended fewer but carefully chosen words. Wise words are a life-giving fountain, wrote Solomon (Proverbs 10:11). They're so rare, they are more valuable than jewels. God Himself declared that what comes from His mouth does not return to Him empty (Isaiah 55:11). Instead, it does what He wants and accomplishes what He intends. That's such a good goal for us!

To restore meaning to our conversations, psychotherapist Mel Schwartz suggests elevating the details of our everyday language. Instead of signing off with a "Love ya" on our phone calls or texts, for instance, he urges us to bring back the "I" and say "I love you." Simple adjustments like this not only communicate sincerity and transparency but are a "deeply . . . emotional offering."[8] Such intention with your words says you cared enough to leave an impression, not just a message.

In a world full of more words than meaning, strive for fewer words and more meaning. Impact is everything.

PROVERBS 17:27-28 NLT

A truly wise person uses few words.... Even fools are thought wise when they keep silent.

PRAYER

When not carefully chosen, my words have only made matters worse. I need Your help in knowing when and how to speak so I can be a blessing to others.

CHOOSING TO TRUST

DAY **37**

The business of acting is very much about choices. You're sent a script, assigned a character, given direction—but once the cameras are rolling, it's up to you to choose how to make that persona come alive. It happens not just through the scenery and costumes, not just through the character's scripted words and actions, but in the nuances that an actor brings to it: posture, voice inflection, facial expressions, gestures, tone, and timing.

The business of real life hinges on our choices as well, though with much higher stakes. We're not striving to entertain or hoping to win awards; we want to come out on the other side with our sanity and faith intact.

One of the things that Jesus said would help most is to submit, or entrust, ourselves to our Father in heaven. Job did this in the most horrible of circumstances. He was as godly as could be, and rich beyond belief, when Satan took everything from him. Nevertheless, his first response after losing his home, his children, his servants, and his livestock was to acknowledge God as God and entrust his life to Him.

Job grieved hard. So hard. And he had a lot of questions about what was happening to him. Yet even in his questions, he did not sin or give up on God, even when those around him urged him to.

Such a powerful testimony! I don't know how he did it, except that God was that real to him. I can only pray that God strengthens my faith so much that, in the day of trial, I, too, choose to trust Him.

JOB 1:21 ESV

The Lord gave, and the Lord has taken away; blessed be the name of the Lord.

PRAYER

Where my faith is weak, Lord, build it strong. Where my priorities have strayed, recenter me on what matters to You. I need You today and every day.

A FAMILY AFFAIR

DAY 38

I'll bet you have a lot of great ways of "ascribing," or recognizing, God's attributes within your household, whether you have roommates, kids, a spouse, or you live alone. Maybe you praise Him with your décor or by saying grace before meals, even in public. I know some people who consistently provide a room for those who are struggling or who welcome local college students around their table for dinners and game nights.

My family likes to do a variety of things as well, but probably one of the most meaningful for us has been to serve others together. Not every family or group of friends can take a mission trip to a foreign country (though if you do get the chance, go for it!), but how about going out "on mission" together and volunteering your time once a month to a local charity? Or brainstorming ways you can team up to "adopt" a widow who might not have loved ones living nearby? Or hosting a simple potluck Friendsgiving each November, where anyone without holiday plans gets invited? Or you could ask your new neighbors to join you for your child's soccer game and a burger afterwards.

Our efforts to bear witness to God extend beyond the ways we serve our church. Anytime we include Him in our lives and households and communities, we are testifying to others about who God is and what it's like to be part of His family. And by this, we make a family affair out of magnifying Him.

1 CHRONICLES 16:28 HCSB

Families of the peoples, ascribe to the LORD glory and strength.

PRAYER

Forgive me for sometimes forgetting how vast Your family is. Show me new ways to include You in the life of my household for Your glory.

TESTIMONY

DAY 39

"What about evolution?" "How do we know the Bible is real?" "If God is a God of love, why did He send His Son to the cross?"

If you're known as "The Christian" among your coworkers and friends, you've probably been asked questions like these by the people you hope to reach with the good news of the gospel. While these questions legitimately deserve a response at some point in our spiritual conversations, I've realized it's pretty rare that somebody comes to Christ as a result of intellectual answers. Usually what's separating them from a relationship with Jesus is something much more personal, whether it's fear of surrendering control, religious wounds from the past, shame for something they've done, or a tragedy that they blame God for.

That's why our stories with Jesus are such powerful testimonies. Sharing our experiences with Him, as well as our own skepticisms when we were first introduced to Him, breaks down walls faster than a PhD in theology ever could. Theology is a wonderful gift to the church, but those outside the church are longing for a touch from Jesus first.

Does that ring true for you? It sure does in my relationships.

Paul's approach to the Corinthians was focused on Christ and told through the lens of relationship and personal experience. History's most effective evangelist was basically saying, "I was afraid about what to say; I knew I didn't have fancy words or arguments to wow you with. All I know is the story of Christ, and His story with me, and His love for us all."

Really, that's all any of us need. That and the Holy Spirit, supplying our words. For our friends and colleagues with ears to hear, God will take care of the rest.

1 CORINTHIANS 2:1-2 NLT

When I first came to you . . . I didn't use lofty words and impressive wisdom to tell you God's secret plan. . . . I decided that while I was with you I would forget everything except Jesus Christ, the one who was crucified.

PRAYER

Lord, You're so good to make a way for Your good news to be heard through the simple sharing of my story with You. Supply me with Your words, not mine, in my spiritual conversations today.

CLEAN SLATE

DAY **40**

I don't know how figure skaters and gymnasts do it. Having points deducted every time you fall has to be intimidating. Viewing their world from the outside makes me so thankful that God skips the points system with us.

Instead of treating us as competitors before a judge or convicts in front of a jury, our heavenly Father treats us as a dad should. That changes the entire picture.

As a parent, have you kept track of how many times your kids have fallen down? Or if you don't have children, did your own parents log how many times you fell? Is the tally in your baby book? No, a loving parent doesn't dwell on the stumbles. A loving parent cares that his or her child gets up again and keeps going.

God doesn't keep an inventory of our sins. That means we don't have to either. Once we repent, that sin is over and done with in His eyes. There's no need for us to look back, because God sure doesn't. Our slates are cleared. Wiped clean. His mercies are new. Every single morning.

It can be hard for us to believe that if we're strapped with shame or a guilty conscience. But those lingering whispers are not from the Lord. Jesus has already paid the debt for those sins, and thus, He has successfully pled our case as our divine Advocate. We've been cleared. Case closed.

The reason it doesn't always feel closed is because our accuser, Satan, loves to kick us while we're down and keep us there. His favorite mirror is the rearview, where what's behind is constantly in our sights. Jesus, however, sets us back on our feet, points us forward, and clears us to run.

Every one of us has things in our past that we'd like to erase. I could reel off several right now. What matters is: Have you sincerely repented of that sin or failure to God? If yes, then do you know what the current headline in heaven says about your case?

ALL CHARGES DROPPED. [YOUR NAME] SET FREE.

Believe it! As John 8:36 says: When Christ sets you free, you are free indeed!

PSALM 130:3-4

If you, Lord, kept a record of sins, Lord, who could stand? But with you there is forgiveness, so that we can, with reverence, serve you.

PRAYER

Jesus, it's because of You that I'm free of my past. Now help me accept and believe it. Moving forward, may I boldly walk in the truth of forgiveness just as boldly as You work on my behalf.

WHAT TO WEAR

DAY 41

One thing I appreciate about chivalrous men is how quick they are to offer their jackets to a woman in chilly weather. They exhibit a principle that is true for any of us: What you put on in the first place, you're more likely to extend to others.

The Good Samaritan (read Luke 10:25–37) was clearly wearing kindness, humility, gentleness, and patience when he walked out of his door that morning. Otherwise, he would have continued on his way, ignoring the crime victim's need, just as the other travelers did. Instead, the Samaritan immediately came to the man's aid—tending his wounds, getting him to a safe place, and paying for his care.

His example makes me take stock of what I'm wearing today. Have I prayerfully consulted with my Maker so that I'm dressed for the "occasion" that He knows I'll be walking into? Stepping out into the world covered in His comfort, compassion, and grace is not only a great look but the best way to make sure others are covered too.

COLOSSIANS 3:12

As God's chosen people, holy and dearly loved, clothe yourselves with compassion, kindness, humility, gentleness and patience.

PRAYER

Clothe me in Your qualities today, Jesus, so that I may eagerly extend Your care and compassion to those whose paths will cross mine.

GO-TIME

DAY **42**

Ladies, I've crossed that threshold, and I'm here to tell you: There is power in forty! At forty years of age, we know ourselves and our bodies so much better. We have a stronger sense of self. We're more sure of our abilities and less bothered by what we can't do. We have a clearer view of our purpose . . . and I could go on and on.

God must think there's something special about forty as well. Pregnancy is typically forty weeks, giving a baby ample time to develop and his or her mom a chance to prepare for the nurturing mission ahead. Moses was on Mount Sinai, receiving the commandments of God, for forty days and nights. The Israelites traveled the desert for forty years until it was time to enter the promised land. Both King David and King Solomon reigned over God's people for forty years. Jesus and John the Baptist spent forty days in the wilderness, where the Holy Spirit readied them for their ministries. And after His resurrection from the dead, Jesus "presented himself alive" to the apostles for forty days, "speaking about the kingdom of God" (Acts 1:3 ESV).

Apparently, God considers forty a training ground for actual go-time. So when the next "forty" in your journey rolls around, embrace it. Anticipate it. Throw a big party if you feel like it. Something momentous is about to happen.

DEUTERONOMY 2:7 ESV

The Lord your God has blessed you in all the work of your hands. He knows your going through this great wilderness. These forty years the Lord your God has been with you.

PRAYER

I needed the reminder that, with You, there is no season to dread. Father God, I look forward to seeing how You'll use the days, weeks, and years ahead to ready me or to send me.

LIFE IN THE SANDBOX

DAY 43

As we grow up, our "playground" changes from sandboxes and schoolyards to workplaces and neighborhoods, but bullies are still in abundance. Thus, the need for common courtesy and consideration toward others never goes away. Those traits may be even more important now that so many of us play in the sandbox of social media.

Being someone in the entertainment business, I'm deeply aware that what I do and say and post is under constant scrutiny. Honestly, though, I'm no different from you. It only takes a few Facebook friends or X followers, and soon enough, you're also being scrutinized.

There's no denying that the culture online trends toward hostility and criticism. Without knowing you or the whole story, people can be pretty quick to judge. I've felt that sting many times, from folks who claim my faith as well as those who believe differently. Once in a while, their words haven't just stung; I've felt outrage and wanted to retaliate, making me even more thankful for Jesus, who proved that turn-the-other-cheek thing is possible.

If it weren't for Him and His forgiveness toward me, I'm sure I'd be a lot more likely to pop off and vent—you know, let people have a piece of my mind. But as followers of Christ, we have alternatives that actually work!

Sometimes we have to walk away from the fight (which may mean no longer reading people's comments); most of the time it's best to hold our tongues; and, every so often, we need to speak up and, with respect, try to help others understand where we're coming from . . . but then let it go.

In the sandbox of life, let's play the way Christ did: Exercise forgiveness, grace, peace. Bless your enemies. Leave vengeance to God. Persist in goodness despite the opposition. And at all times, as far as it depends on us, bring the peace.

ROMANS 12:18

If it is possible, as far as it depends on you, live at peace with everyone.

PRAYER

You know better than anyone, Jesus, that life in the adult sandbox can be rough. I'm looking to You for patience, a peaceful response, and grace toward others.

IDENTITY THEFT

DAY

As sure as you're reading this, Satan is trying to steal your identity—your spiritual identity, that is. You know he's on the prowl when the messages you're hearing or telling yourself are saying that your worth is in anything or anyone besides Christ.

The Enemy makes me so mad! What a liar!

In describing our adversary in John 8:44, Jesus essentially said, "You want to know when Satan is lying? Every time he opens his mouth!" Lies are his native tongue, Jesus explained; Satan is the "father of lies," the originator of lying. Not only that, he is "a murderer" and has been "from the beginning."

All of this tells us that our nemesis is a lifelong criminal who has been targeting the sons and daughters of God since time began. Thankfully, Scripture teaches us how to recognize him so that we can avoid being one of his victims.

Anytime you're getting whispers that your worth is based on who you please, what you accomplish, who you're hanging with, how you look, or what you own . . . tell the Enemy you're on to him. Reject his lies out loud and counter them with the words of truth you find in Scripture. I do that sometimes to guide my head straight.

Where Satan is set on robbing us of our identities and our joy, Jesus offers us life overflowing. You and I are daughters of the King with royal blood in our veins. We belong to Christ alone. And according to Him, once a princess, always a princess.

JOHN 10:10

The thief comes only to steal and kill and destroy; I have come that they may have life, and have it to the full.

PRAYER

Don't let me forget that my identity is in You, Jesus. Remind me that I'm a princess within Your forever kingdom, a member of Your royal family. No one can take that away from me.

HOW I LOVE THEE

DAY 45

Surely there's been a time, in class or conversation, when you've heard the famous opening lines of Elizabeth Barrett Browning's forty-third sonnet:

How do I love thee? Let me count the ways.
I love thee to the depth and breadth and height
My soul can reach . . .

The famous poet concludes:

I love thee with the breath,
Smiles, tears, of all my life; and, if God choose,
I shall but love thee better after death.

I wonder if this sonnet, written back in 1845 or 1846, has struck such a timeless chord because it so beautifully expresses affection for the one who is loved instead of the beloved's deeds or qualities. As nice as gratitude and appreciation are, anyone who's ever been in love knows that loving good things about someone isn't the same as loving them. Gratitude and appreciation are at least a little transactional, involving some benefit to us. The real thing, loving the person behind all those qualities, is outright transformational, for you and for them.

So it's good for us to occasionally return to the heart of our relationship with God and reaffirm: *I love You, God, not just Your power that protects me. Your gifts to me are wonderful, but You are my very life and breath.*

I'll be taking a few minutes today to express my love for the One who has captured my heart. I hope you will too. Poets or not, we can journal it, sing it, shout it, dance it, pray it, play it, paint it, or meditate on it. Or we could offer Browning's own words to Jesus or any of the beautiful expressions in the Psalms. Let's just pause to count the many, many ways we love Him.

PSALM 73:25-26 ESV

Whom have I in heaven but you? And there is nothing on earth that I desire besides you. My flesh and my heart may fail, but God is the strength of my heart and my portion forever.

PRAYER

Jesus, I love You. With all my heart, soul, mind, and strength, I love You. From the depths of me, each and every way, I love You.

FOR DOUBTING THOMASES EVERYWHERE

DAY **46**

Has anyone ever called you a "doubting Thomas"? I feel for the guy because, after rereading his experience in John 20 and then digging into the context a little more, I think he's often judged unfairly. I doubt he's alone . . .

One of Jesus' original twelve disciples, Thomas, enjoyed hours of fellowship with his Teacher during Christ's time on earth. Having also witnessed many of His miracles firsthand, Thomas and the other disciples must've been especially heartbroken at the events of the previous week—that first Easter week. I can imagine that Jesus' betrayal by one of their own, followed by His brutal beating and crucifixion, had not only been traumatizing for His friends to watch, but also that they were grieving deeply at all the injustice and the loss. What's more, the disciples were hiding out behind locked doors out of fear that the Jews might come after them. So Thomas was devastated, spent, and afraid—a hard time for anybody to be full of faith.

Putting myself in those shoes, I can better understand his reaction to the other disciples' report. "We have seen the Lord!" they exclaimed, barely able to contain their excitement. Thomas wasn't buying it. My guess? He didn't want to get his hopes up. The thought of one more disappointment was more than he could bear. So in what was probably an act of self-protection, he remarked that unless he could touch and see Christ's wounds from the cross, "I will not believe" (v. 25).

Fast-forward a week. Christ's disciples were together again, still behind locked doors, and this time, Thomas was with them. Jesus miraculously appeared among them and said, "Peace be with you!" Then He turned to Thomas, in a tone that a lot of pastors read as a gentle invitation rather than a reprimand, and said: "Put your finger here; see my hands. Reach out your hand and put it into my side. Stop doubting and believe" (vv. 26–27).

Jesus knew Thomas. He knew this disciple to be inquisitive and sometimes bold, not passive. And as Jesus expected, Thomas got it, exclaiming, "My Lord and my God!" (v. 28).

To me, Thomas's faith comes across, well, pretty normal: sometimes brimming, sometimes ebbing, yet steadily devoted to Jesus. Our short-lived struggles with skepticism aren't our proudest moments, but they're as ripe for redemption as any. Especially the struggles arising from suffering or grief.

In Thomas's crisis of belief, Jesus made Himself known. For you and for me, doubt can be that bridge where our sight finally meets faith.

MARK 9:24

Immediately the boy's father exclaimed, "I do believe; help me overcome my unbelief!"

PRAYER

While I do sometimes question what You're doing or what circumstances mean, thank You for knowing that I'm no less devoted to You. In those areas where I'm struggling with doubt right now, I affirm my belief in You, but I also pray, Jesus, that You'll help my unbelief.

GUARDED

DAY 47

As you're reading your Bible, it's always worth noticing the words tucked within the Word, paying attention to the surprises that are hiding in plain sight. One example is today's feature verse. Paul's prayer for the Christians in Philippi was that the peace of God would guard their hearts and minds in Christ. Till now, I've never thought of peace as a defense, a protection. But it is. A good bodyguard has nothing on the peace of God, because His peace shields our hearts and minds—the two places where, supernaturally speaking, we are most vulnerable to attack.

How can this be? I can think of a few ways that divine peace protects us . . .

For one, peace helps us keep a cool head in adversarial situations so that we can respond with the grace and words of the Holy Spirit instead of what we'd really like to say. Peace also can supply us with compassion for those who are opposing us. Instead of just hearing their words, God sometimes gives us a glimpse into what's happening inside them. That glimpse of their fear or pain won't always ease our anger immediately, but once a little empathy trickles in, our hurt may start to evaporate, helping us to forgive. Finally, peace produces contentment, whether circumstances are going our way or not. I'm not saying I've never felt disappointed or afraid while enduring hardship, but the peace of Christ prevents us from lingering in those emotions long-term.

As you add your own ideas to this starter list, keep it close to your heart. God's super-peace is real, and through it, He is keeping watch over us.

PHILIPPIANS 4:7 NASB

The peace of God, which surpasses all comprehension, will guard your hearts and minds in Christ Jesus.

PRAYER

Let Your peace be my shield and fortress today, Jesus, from head to toe.

MARATHON MINDSET

DAY **48**

My dear friend and co-star Andrea Barber, known to *Full House* and *Fuller House* fans as Kimmy Gibbler, got into running several years ago and convinced me to do a few races with her. I enjoyed them, but compared to the interval and resistance training I usually do, I found that running long distances required a very different mindset.

The same could be said for our spiritual journey. To understand the life of faith as an endurance race changes our approach in some key ways. First, it means instilling long-term strategies that will build us up spiritually. Disciplines such as Bible reading, prayer, and Scripture memorization. The daily vitamins of God's Word. Energy boosters such as worship, fellowship with other believers, and ongoing acts of service.

Second, understanding our faith as a long-distance race means we can better manage our expectations. When I head into a movie production, for instance, I know it's going to require longer hours, a higher scene count per day, more wardrobe, hair, and makeup changes, and more lines to memorize than a TV episode that wraps in a four-day week. Additionally, being on location involves filming outdoors, where we're subject to weather and other circumstances beyond human control. These additional demands and obstacles aren't surprises; they come with the territory of shooting a movie.

Similarly, when things don't go exactly as we'd hoped in our Christian life or when we experience delays that God is directing, a marathon mindset helps. With eternity as our prize, crossing the finish line takes precedence over momentary distractions and frustrations. Best of all, the joy of the Lord grows. We get the "runner's high" that only God delivers, and it stays with us, all the way to the winner's stand!

1 CORINTHIANS 9:24–25

Do you not know that in a race all the runners run, but only one gets the prize? Run in such a way as to get the prize. Everyone who competes in the games goes into strict training. They do it to get a crown that will not last, but we do it to get a crown that will last forever.

PRAYER

Dear God, train me to run the race and stay in it for the long haul. I trust You to fill me with increasing joy as I go and to make me stronger mile after mile.

SEIZE THIS DAY

DAY 49

The movie *Dead Poets Society*, which starred the late Robin Williams as an instructor at a private boys' school, is known for one of film history's most famous lines. I won't spoil the details for you if you haven't seen it, but on the first day of class, Williams's character, Mr. Keating, dramatically and memorably urges his students to heed the words of a long-ago poet. "Seize the day," he tells them. "Make your lives extraordinary."

That message is on God's heart for every one of us. We've all heard people say things like, "I'm just killing time until I'm married/have kids/my career takes off," or whatever they believe their next thing is. Yet God has valuable plans for you and for me during the next twenty-four hours—and in the days and weeks after that. So to say we intend to kill some time means we're missing out on all the treasure He has tucked away in this day.

I'm not saying anything to you here that I'm not saying to myself. No new day is something to waste; we will never have another one exactly like it. It's twenty-four hours given to us to care for just as wisely as a pile of diamonds we found stashed in our great-grandmother's jewelry box.

Time is a limited commodity that, invested carefully, can make us rich multiple times over—relationally, emotionally, spiritually. Whatever you do with this day, don't kill it, and don't let it slip through your fingers. Make it memorable. Make it mean something. Make it extraordinary.

EPHESIANS 5:15-16

Be very careful, then, how you live—not as unwise but as wise, making the most of every opportunity, because the days are evil.

PRAYER

Lord, the last thing I want is to waste a good thing. I promise to seize this day. Now help me to live it for all it's worth.

DANCING WITH THE SPIRIT

DAY 50

Competing on *Dancing with the Stars* was unquestionably the hardest I've ever worked physically. I had to give it my all because . . . I really didn't know how to dance. Fortunately, I was paired with a great partner, and I was willing to work my dancing shoes off, and it ended up being a great experience.

It turns out, I haven't always known how to rest either. I've needed a strong Partner to walk me through the steps and teach me to flow freely with "the unforced rhythms of grace."

The one pointer I can give you from *DWTS* and my journey with Jesus is, follow your Partner's lead. When He tells you to slow down, ease up. When He tells you to run, go like a gazelle. When He says, "Turn here" or "Leap, I'll catch you," believe Him. And when He says, "Wait," stand still. You can trust the Spirit's lead in all things.

MATTHEW 11:28-30 MSG

Are you tired? Worn out? Burned out on religion? Come to me. Get away with me and you'll recover your life. I'll show you how to take a real rest. Walk with me and work with me—watch how I do it. Learn the unforced rhythms of grace. I won't lay anything heavy or ill-fitting on you. Keep company with me and you'll learn to live freely and lightly.

PRAYER

You so graciously lead me through each and every day, knowing my next move before I even know to move. I'm honored to be Your partner. Lead on; Lord, I'll do my best to follow You.

EVERGREEN

DAY 51

Out of curiosity, I did a little botanical research to see how Jeremiah's imagery in today's verse lined up with science. (No judgment, okay? Having to argue for intelligent design and other biblical truths on national television will do that to you.) Let me share a few real-world parallels that I found.

Just as Jeremiah indicates, a tree's growth is influenced as much by its environment as genetics. That environment determines everything from its height to its ability to provide shade, shelter, food, and fuel.

Also, for any tree, root integrity and health are of utmost importance. According to botanists, if the roots are damaged at all, it's a potential for hazard—the likelihood that it will die or be brought down by natural causes such as storms, pests, or disease—rises substantially. On the other hand, if a tree with healthy roots is situated near a water source, it will be particularly drought-resistant.

The roots make life possible. They also give stability so that a tree can grow strong and tall. Scientists say that for all the beauty you see aboveground, an even more expansive root system almost always exists belowground.

What an inspiring picture of how our lives can be!

As our roots in God grab a wider and deeper hold, we are able to push higher and straighter, like a California redwood. Add His light and living water, and it's possible for us to thrive in every season, being evergreen for decades to come.

JEREMIAH 17:7–8

Blessed is the one who trusts in the Lord, whose confidence is in him. They will be like a tree planted by the water that sends out its roots by the stream. It does not fear when heat comes; its leaves are always green. It has no worries in a year of drought and never fails to bear fruit.

PRAYER

I love the truth of Your Word, Lord, and how it so accurately reflects the realities we live in. Grow me sturdy and strong like a redwood, for You and others. And make my faith evergreen.

FEAR FACTOR

DAY 52

Were you a fan of the TV show *Fear Factor*? It was a reality competition involving different physical challenges—some of them hair-raising (traversing a tightrope between two buildings), some of them gross (eating rotten food), and some of them just plain difficult (holding your breath in a water tank while hanging upside down Houdini-style).

Sadly, most people don't need a TV show to tap their adrenaline; life has enough fear of its own. We moms are pretty good at dreaming up what troubles our kids can get into, right? We don't own the market, though. You can be eight, eighteen, or eighty-five and be bound up by worry or dread.

God knew we would be prone to fear; after all, we live in a fallen world. So it makes sense that He included almost as many "Do not fear" verses in the Bible as there are days in a year. We need to be reminded of His strength and ever-present help that often.

Today, if you start to feel afraid, why not do more than read some of His fear-fighting words to you? Insert your name into them and recite them out loud. Then, imagine sitting in the lap of your strong, protective, loving Father as He gently whispers those words to you personally.

Can you hear Him? *"Do not fear, beloved. I am with you. I am making you strong."*

ISAIAH 41:10

Do not fear, for I am with you; do not be dismayed, for I am your God. I will strengthen you and help you; I will uphold you with my righteous right hand.

PRAYER

Oh, how I long to breathe out my fear and breathe in Your calm, Daddy. Reassure me that You are right here with me as many times as I need it today.

DESIGNER LABEL

DAY **53**

I make no secret of my love for style and fashion. Even as a child actor, I liked the wardrobe part, not just the performing. So you won't hear me complain about getting to dress up and play Cinderella for an evening every once in a while at a red-carpet event.

For all the times I don't attend the awards shows, I still tune in from my couch along with the rest of America to see what everyone is wearing.

Besides the gowns and tuxes, those events are known for the throng of media. I'm not exaggerating when I say cameras are literally everywhere you look. And each of those cameras represents another audience watching from somewhere.

Hollywood's red-carpet world may seem a million miles away from your own, but in the most important sense, it's not. As God's anointed people, you and I have experienced one of His signature makeovers and the new stylings that go with it.

Our Designer's label is distinctive. As one of His "stars" who ventures out and draws attention to Him every day, I want to be sure that I'm wearing Him well, exhibiting the modesty, elegance, and class that mark His brand.

Biblically, God offers a few guidelines for those times when the world is watching:

He instructs me to get rid of my dingy, old, ill-fitting clothes and put on the new, tailored gowns that He has made for me (Colossians 3:9–10; 12–14).

He fashions me with the strength and dignity that belong on a virtuous woman (Proverbs 31:25).

He prompts me to stand up straight with my heart and mind focused on things above, not on the things of this earth (Colossians 3:1–2).

And He urges me to smile, reminding me of His light within, which turns people's attention to Him.

Whatever we do, girls, we do it all in the name of Jesus. The world is taking note of what we're wearing and Who we're wearing. Now's our chance to go beyond a fashion statement. Let's wear Him with pride today.

MATTHEW 5:14, 16 NKJV

You are the light of the world. . . . Let your light so shine before men, that they may see your good works and glorify your Father in heaven.

PRAYER

I'm so excited to be wearing Your name, Jesus. Help me to not only make a good impression on others but to represent how wonderful You are to everyone who's watching.

SITTING IT OUT

DAY **54**

We're living in a culture where almost no one hesitates to say what's on their mind. In the court of public opinion, every topic is fair game; every comment carries weight. So Paul's sound advice to a young pastor is a good word for us today.

Social media, office politics, bickering among friends or family members or within a church—petty arguments are popping up around us almost constantly, like a never-ending game of Whac-A-Mole. Anytime they do, God invites us to pause, take a breath, and consciously decide: *Am I going to join in or sit this one out?*

We do have that choice. And according to Paul, it's a choice worth taking seriously.

Conflict is essentially a bicycle built for two. When one person steps off and quits the quarrel ride, you can guarantee that, unless another rider comes along, the bike won't be going much farther.

There are undoubtedly situations and topics that deserve our full (and patient) engagement. Paul's own life bore this out. But for those little opinions that only stir up trouble or the nitpicking over inconsequential things? We can leave those fight-starters alone, lest they become fire-starters.

2 TIMOTHY 2:23-24 NLT

Don't get involved in foolish, ignorant arguments that only start fights. A servant of the Lord must not quarrel but must be kind to everyone . . . and be patient with difficult people.

PRAYER

Though sometimes I'm tempted to spout my opinion, give me the grace to hold my tongue and walk away from the pettiness before it starts.

PRAYING FOR ME?

DAY 55

Jesus prays for us. How incredible is that? The One who never sleeps is at the right hand of God in heaven, constantly praying with us and for us.

We were also in His thoughts and prayers in the hours preceding His crucifixion. Among His requests on our behalf were that we would know and accept the words we've heard from Him, that our heavenly Father would protect us from the Evil One by the power of Christ's name while we are in this world, that we would experience utmost joy, and that as Christians would be unified in our faith and exhibit God's love to the world until we one day reunite with Jesus in heaven (Luke 11:28; John 17:15; John 16:24; John 17:20–24).

Jesus is still praying today. He's praying for you and your church family to be protected, preserved in the truth, and filled with joy. He is also praying for the people you know and love who don't yet know Him.

Whatever you're up against right now, He's praying you through it. At this very moment, Jesus has you on His mind.

ROMANS 8:34 HCSB

Christ Jesus is the One who died, but even more, has been raised; He also is at the right hand of God and intercedes for us.

PRAYER

Today, I am reminded of how intimately close You are. I know I'm not alone; I'm in the presence of my King.

TRAINING GROUND

DAY **56**

Ask any professional athlete or Olympic medalist about the hours of practice they put in, and you'll hear answers that amount to years and years, if not a lifetime. Mastery isn't developed overnight. Yet almost all the professional athletes I know (hey, I even married one!) will tell you, "The countless hours were worth the reward."

It's no different with our spiritual training. Godliness requires the determined, disciplined effort of an athlete. And the more we practice, the more we will be rewarded in all ways. Isn't that great? Our training yields a huge return on investment, both now and in eternity!

British pastor Charles Spurgeon once classified the benefits of godliness in this life as "peace of mind, peace with God, contentment, and happiness of spirit."[9] I can't think of any greater outcomes than those four things, can you? And they're only a foretaste of our future rewards (plural!) in heaven.

Though it does take time, sweat, and some tears, too, the hours we spend training in godliness are never a waste of time. So let's go for it, ladies! I'm feeling like a good workout just about now. How about you?

1 TIMOTHY 4:7-8

Train yourself to be godly. For physical training is of some value, but godliness has value for all things, holding promise for both the present life and the life to come.

PRAYER

Increase my discipline, my motivation, and my desire for all the things that will make me more like You. I'm going for the gold, Coach. Lead the way to victory!

OWNING IT

DAY 57

Dog lover that I am, it's funny to me how the littlest dogs can sometimes be the most aggressive. Have you noticed that? They might weigh five pounds and stand no taller than your shins. Doesn't matter. They'll take on dogs five times their size or go after two-hundred-pound humans, owning it with every cell in their body.

Little dogs often think they're big dogs that rule the yard. Why big dogs will go along with this, in spite of the pip-squeak nipping at their ankles, I'll never know. But they acknowledge as pack leader whichever dog asserts itself enough.

That's not so different from Satan's MO. He goes around roaring at us as if he's the king of the jungle, but he doesn't have nearly the power that he pretends to—unless we buy in.

You and I can stand firm amid the growls and threats because we know who the real King is. His power is unmistakable: "The Mighty One, God, the LORD, speaks and summons the earth from the rising of the sun to where it sets" (Psalm 50:1); He "rides across the highest heavens" and "thunders with mighty voice. . . . [His] majesty is over Israel, [His] power is in the heavens" (Psalm 68:33–34). "Clouds are the dust of his feet" (Nahum 1:3).

The Leader we follow rules the yard as if He owns it and protects us fiercely as if He owns us. Because He does. We have no one and nothing to fear.

2 CORINTHIANS 1:21-22

Now it is God who makes both us and you stand firm in Christ. He anointed us, set his seal of ownership on us, and put his Spirit in our hearts as a deposit, guaranteeing what is to come.

PRAYER

Lord, if I start to cower at another voice today, would You prompt me about it? I don't care how loud those voices are; I intend to listen only to Yours.

KEEP IT SIMPLE

DAY 58

Giving cheerfully isn't necessarily about giving big; it's a matter of giving well, from the heart. Sometimes that means donating or tithing money, but more often, life affords us simple opportunities to give of our time and ourselves in valuable ways.

With our already-packed calendars, simple is a blessing! It means we can do things more often, but with way less stress. To me, that amounts to a whole lot of joy coming our way.

The possibilities are endless. Instead of throwing a huge party with extravagant decorations, how about inviting your next-door neighbors over for soup and sandwiches? Nothing fancy, just a little hospitality from the heart. Or you could take five minutes and send someone you love a list of "The Top 10 Reasons I'm Crazy About You."

Other simple ideas? Post a compliment about an unsung hero you know whom you "caught in the act" of doing a good thing. Tip your waiter or waitress a little extra for going the extra mile to give you good service. Or pick a flower from your garden, drop it in one of those bud vases that I just know you have sitting around the house, and surprise the widow down the street with a quick hello and a hug.

It doesn't take big money to bless somebody in a big way. Just be thoughtful. Do something extra that puts a smile on your face. Chances are, it will put a smile on someone else's face too.

2 CORINTHIANS 9:6-7 NASB

The one who sows generously will also reap generously. Each one must do just as he has decided in his heart, not reluctantly or under compulsion, for God loves a cheerful giver.

PRAYER

Lord, keep me on the lookout for the variety of ways I can bless the people I meet. And help me to give with a joyful heart.

THE PITS

DAY 59

There's one thing everyone can say about a pit: The view is miserable. Walls in front of you. Darkness and stale air around you. The shape and size of yours may be different from the next person's, but the depths are enough to dishearten anyone.

A quick overview of the Bible reveals how many, many of our brothers and sisters of the past could relate to the types of places we find ourselves in. Joseph was dumped in a pit by his own brothers. Job was buried in grief and loss. Daniel and three of his friends were faced with predators and fire in theirs. Several of the disciples were thrown behind bars. Naomi, widowed in a foreign land during a time of famine, felt abandoned by God. Hannah was despondent in her barrenness. And the writers of the Psalms spoke openly of pits of doubt and fear and oppression at the hands of their enemies.

Human nature in these times is to look down and wallow in the slime of our circumstances, sinking ever deeper into the mud. Our better choice is to do as God's servants did: Look up, cry out to God, and trust Him for our deliverance. He may intervene directly or through the aid of others; either way, He brings us to solid ground and a new song.

What's your status today? Are you sick and tired? Broken? Feeling left behind? Call a heavenly 911. Help is on its way.

PSALM 40:1-3

I waited patiently for the LORD; he turned to me and heard my cry. He lifted me out of the slimy pit, out of the mud and mire; he set my feet on a rock and gave me a firm place to stand. He put a new song in my mouth, a hymn of praise to our God.

PRAYER

Though my suffering at times has caught me off guard, I've seen You turn my pits into sacred spaces where You met me. Like the many believers before me, meet me where I am, sustained by hope in You while I await the new song You're creating in me.

OPEN ARMS

DAY 60

God is mad at us this time! The people of Israel must have said that to themselves repeatedly as a nation in Old Testament times. And it is true. Ancient Israel's rebellion often aroused the Lord's anger, just as a teenager's defiance upsets his or her parents.

I can appreciate that God didn't hide it; He admitted His disappointment at their choices. He was transparent about His displeasure. But alongside those strong emotions, He expressed His eagerness to forgive.

Today, you may be legitimately feeling, *God is mad at me this time!* because of something you've done. Please don't run from Him—I've tried, and it never brings peace.

Our sin does make God mad, but remember: Beyond the anger is grief. The grief of a Father who, though betrayed and wounded, still loves. Who still wants His relationship with you restored and reconciled.

Rather than hiding from Him in fear, as Adam and Eve did, or getting frustrated and punishing yourself, just tell Him you're sorry. Then turn wholeheartedly from that sin and run to Him. The One who is slow to anger and abounding in love is waiting with open arms.

JOEL 2:12-13

"Even now," declares the Lord, "return to me with all your heart, with fasting and weeping and mourning." Rend your heart and not your garments. Return to the Lord your God, for he is gracious and compassionate, slow to anger and abounding in love, and he relents from sending calamity.

PRAYER

God, I'm sorry for rebelling against You and running away in fear. Hold me tight in Your arms until my fear goes away.

ON PURPOSE

DAY 61

We're at our best when we're living from the inside out. By that, I mean living on purpose in our pursuits rather than letting the world decide for us.

It's not easy, is it? You and I are constantly being bombarded with demands on our time, our attentions, and our intentions. If our electronic devices aren't tugging at us, our calendars are; and if not our calendars, then commercials and ads; and if not those, it's the people we're with every day who need or want something from us.

Not all of these requests are bad. In fact, any number of them may be worthwhile. Nevertheless, we owe it to God and ourselves to figure out who we are so that we can say yes—and no—for maximum impact.

Our primary purpose as people of faith is to glorify God. And our secondary priorities, as I call them, are all the ways we get to glorify God. You may be running your own business, working for somebody else and pursuing a side hustle, volunteering in your community, putting in lots of hours at your church, or serving as the CEO of your household. In every situation, let your God-given purpose and priorities be your guide. And invite God to partner with you in these pursuits. He is ready, willing, and able to empower you for every good work He has purposed in you.

EPHESIANS 3:16-17

I pray that out of his glorious riches he may strengthen you with power through his Spirit in your inner being, so that Christ may dwell in your hearts through faith.

PRAYER

Of all the demands that will come my way today, God, please show me which ones You want me to respond to and which ones to turn down. I'm excited to be partnering with You in the adventure we're on!

HEALING RAIN

DAY 62

Ugh, those extra-busy seasons of life . . . I enjoy being as productive as the next person, but I don't miss the mega-packed months-in-succession where there's no breathing room.

You've lived it, I know. Functioning on caffeine and adrenaline. Putting out fires. Doing lots of good for others. Juggling work and home and church commitments. All the while you're running dry. Or in my case, stagnating.

Logic says, the constant motion should keep our internal waters fed and our creativity flowing. Experience shows, those are the seasons that I'm most likely to turn stagnant spiritually and otherwise.

The last time this happened to me, I decided to ask one thing of the Lord in place of a New Year's resolution. My prayer was, "God, please help me grow." I had to double down on my purpose, say no to some things, and get time away with my family and with God. Slowly but surely, the muck drained off. God's restoring rain soaked in. And the Holy Spirit turned up new ground in my heart, bringing back my joy.

I don't know what invigorating change the Holy Spirit may be inviting you to right now, but God is absolutely with you in that pursuit. Is it to repentance and a relationship with Jesus as your Savior? A fresh wind of faith or a greater passion for God? Is there a place in your heart that you've left untouched due to shame or disappointment or some hurt? Could you use some healing rain there today?

In Isaiah 43:19, the Lord says, "Watch closely: I am preparing something new; it's happening now, even as I speak, and you're about to see it. I am preparing a way through the desert; waters will flow where there had been none" (The Voice). Whatever growth you're seeking, run your heart's desire by Him so the two of you can work out a simple plan of action. Once you have that, do it—little by little, day by day.

Things are about to change. Do you see it coming? Healing rain is on its way.

HOSEA 10:12 ESV

Sow for yourselves righteousness; reap steadfast love; break up your fallow ground, for it is the time to seek the LORD, that he may come and rain righteousness upon you.

PRAYER

I'm watching closely, praying for Your refreshing, God. Send relief. Wash over me, restoring my joy.

TURN UP THE LIGHT

DAY **63**

No spiritual transformation in history compares to the apostle Paul's. Within only three years of his conversion, he went from persecuting Christians to their death to debating religious teachers and astonishing listeners with his fearless preaching of Jesus as the Son of God.

He could do these things because he immersed himself in the teaching of Christ as a new believer. "I received my message from no human source," he explained later. "I received it by direct revelation from Jesus Christ" (Galatians 1:12 NLT).

Like us, Paul didn't have the advantage of knowing Jesus while he walked the earth; he had what we have: the Scriptures, the Holy Spirit, and a relationship with Christ. That was his seminary, so to speak. Through that training, God equipped Paul to instruct pastors, plant churches, and evangelize the unsaved all over the ancient world—and the ripple effect of his ministry reaches us today.

His experience excites me so much! What might God do through us as we invest time in Bible reading and prayer?

Clearly, God doesn't care how long we've been a Christian. He doesn't disqualify us because we're in the early days of our faith. He can teach us, purpose us, use us from the start of our salvation—or at any point thereafter.

His Word makes the difference, illuminating who Jesus is and God's incredible plans for us. Nothing else turns up the light so quickly.

PSALM 119:98–99, 130 NLT

Your commands make me wiser than my enemies, for they are my constant guide. Yes, I have more insight than my teachers, for I am always thinking of your laws. . . . The teaching of your word gives light, so even the simple can understand.

PRAYER

What a gift Your Word is! Knowing that the Holy Spirit will take Your teachings and enlighten my soul every time I open my Bible is a game changer.

MAKING THE LIST

DAY **64**

More and more magazines are publishing lists—sometimes yearly, sometimes more often than that—of the influencers within their demographic, from the best companies or colleges to the world's wealthiest people to the top young entrepreneurs. I'm guessing those issues see very strong sales because almost everyone loves a good list to dish over and debate.

Those influencing entities or individuals usually have name recognition. They're considered VIPs. The real meaning of the word *influence*, however, has very little to do with status and everything to do with one's effect on others. "*Influence*, we get that word from Latin. It comes from two words in Latin: *in* and *flow*," explains popular author and CEO O. S. Hawkins. "So the word picture is just this mighty river, flowing crystal clear, vibrant current, and into it come these little tributaries and streams, make their way into it and they're carried away in its flow. That's what influence is."[10]

Jesus didn't choose His team of twelve disciples from the halls of government in His day, and I doubt He would be looking to Hollywood or Wall Street or ESPN today. He found His influencers on Main Street and on the shorelines. They were ordinary people with ordinary occupations by society's standards. Yet their ministry efforts in partnership with Him launched a movement that has reached every corner of the world in every generation.

Jesus is still calling disciples today from Main Street and beyond. A few of them have name recognition, but most of them come from the back roads and shorelines and the back rows of church pews.

You are on His list. He knows your name, and He plans for you to deeply "inflow" your gifts and wisdom and love to others. You're an influencer, whether you know it or not. Your impact is being felt, whether or not you ever make the headlines.

JOHN 7:38 HCSB

The one who believes in Me, as the Scripture has said, will have streams of living water flow from deep within him.

PRAYER

For all the godly men and women who have poured into my life, I thank You. I'm intent on being an influencer in its true sense, reaching others for You.

ROCK DROP

DAY **65**

Any weight is capable of hindering our faith, but the one that causes the most drag in our step just might be unforgiveness.

I really can't think of a tougher command than "Forgive." It always seems to have layers to it. Complicated layers that are painful to work through and hard to shake off.

Author Nicole Johnson calls the process of forgiveness "dropping the rock."[11] Exercising our forgiveness muscles may feel uncomfortable at first. Yet, just as in our physical workouts, the soreness of exercising rarely used muscles is a signal that they—and we—are getting stronger.

I can't say enough about the impact a personal trainer makes either. To have someone who pushes me and shows me how to work my muscles correctly ensures my success. In this vital area, there's no better or more qualified trainer than Jesus. Not only has He forgiven us for all those times we've hurt Him, but He is the elite example of forgiving others.

Jesus was lied about, gossiped about, publicly maligned, accused of things He didn't do or say, thrown under the bus so that the "throwers" could save themselves, and subjected to verbal abuse and physical torture. He never deserved any of it, and most of these offenders never bothered to apologize. Even so, among His dying words were, "Father, forgive them; for they know not what they do" (Luke 23:34 KJV).

Jesus knew the freedom of dropping the rock. So can we.

To keep carrying rocks of resentment doesn't hurt the other person; it only slows us down. Dropping these stones is like losing the weighted jacket from a workout. Once you get rid of it, you instantly feel like you can jump higher and run faster than ever before.

Thanks to Christ, it's true. A heart that has dumped its load of bitterness is unhindered and free. Nothing can hold you back.

HEBREWS 12:1-2 NLT

Let us strip off every weight that slows us down, especially the sin that so easily trips us up. And let us run with endurance the race God has set before us. We do this by keeping our eyes on Jesus, the champion who initiates and perfects our faith.

PRAYER

You know I've been carrying around grudges and resentments for way too long. Jesus, free me of this weight. Grant me the courage to drop the rocks and leave in Your hands those who have hurt me.

LOOK FOR THE EXITS

DAY 66

I say, if we're going to learn vigilance, let's learn from the experts—the people who protect and defend others for a living. Our heroes in the armed services and in law enforcement are trained to look for an escape route whenever they enter a room, just in case. To survey our surroundings emotionally and spiritually as we enter a temptation-prone setting—a party, for instance, or a business trip with colleagues—is a great idea spiritually. Where are the hazards in that place? Who should we be wary of? How can we stay on the alert and limit our exposure to trouble?

You won't read of one incident in the Bible where a believer wasn't given an out. God always supplies an alternative to sin and sometimes more than one. So we're wise to decide where we're headed should the emergency alarms go off. People may be doing crazy or dangerous things around you. Save others if you can, but be sure to save yourself as well.

Vigilance and forethought are two of God's top life-preserving skills. We can't always predict where temptation will flare up, but we know it will eventually, and we usually have a pretty good idea of which areas of our lives are most susceptible. Locating the nearest exit is a strong defense. Plus, having an exit strategy takes much of the heat out of the moment and off ourselves.

Less heat equals a calmer head.

Less heat equals the strength to run for cover.

Summed up: less heat equals a way happier life.

PROVERBS 4:23 ESV

Keep your heart with all vigilance, for from it flow the springs of life.

PRAYER

Lord, as I reflect on my years with You, I'm thankful for all Your escape paths that have led me to safety. I'm also sorry for the times I chose not to follow the exits You provided. Use those past experiences to increase my vigilance in the battle for my heart.

DAIRY-FREE FAITH

DAY 67

With all due respect to the cows of the world, can you imagine an adult surviving on milk alone? Milk is the perfect food source when you're an infant with no teeth for chewing. But as time goes on, every baby—in order to grow into adulthood—needs to leave the dairy diet behind and start cutting his or her teeth on solid foods.

The believers being addressed in the book of Hebrews had been Christians for so long that they could have been, should have been, teaching others the meat of the gospel. Instead, they themselves needed a refresher course in the ABCs. Not the Bible basics of adult Sunday school; evidently those were too much for them. Even children's church was above their heads. These full-grown believers were still hanging out in the nursery!

No Christian I know wants that. So what's the mark of someone who has graduated to solid food and is steadily progressing toward spiritual adulthood? One Bible translation says it's being able to both "distinguish" what is against divine or human law and carefully "discriminate" what is "morally good and noble" (Hebrews 5:14 AMPC).

The detailed wording indicates that being a grown-up in God's eyes goes beyond understanding what's clearly commanded. After all, most five-year-olds have a pretty good sense of right and wrong. So we haven't arrived just because we can distinguish the rotten milk from the good stuff. In fact, we're only getting started!

True spiritual maturity also entails developing a discriminating sense of taste, where we learn to choose what's better . . . and then ultimately, with practice, hone our skills to discern the highest, or noblest, good in a situation. In food terms, we learn how to pick the finest cut from a platter full of filet mignon.

    The Bible calls this wisdom, a skill we gain primarily through practice. By continually putting the guidance of Scripture and the Holy Spirit into action, we learn to handle the Word well . . . and before we know it, we're adulting! Thinking like adults. Seeing the world through mature eyes. Acting our age in the very best of ways.

HEBREWS 5:13-14 NLT

Someone who lives on milk is still an infant and doesn't know how to do what is right. Solid food is for those who are mature, who through training have the skill to recognize the difference between right and wrong.

PRAYER

God, I don't have any interest in staying a spiritual baby. Increase my hunger for You and, with it, my understanding. I promise to put into practice the things You teach me.

LOVE LETTER

DAY **68**

The Bible is a love letter from start to finish. It has everything! From poems and song lyrics to faithful vows to God's ambitions and dreams for His life with you and me. The One who adores us shares page after page of His unconditional love.

Whew, that's pretty remarkable!

In our techie era, while we've lost some of the art of letter writing, I'm pretty sure that almost every one of us has a box or drawer somewhere that preserves the words of our loved ones as keepsakes that we can go back to anytime we want. People's kindnesses and encouragements via text or email are keepers, for sure. But their letters or handwritten cards? Priceless.

As soon as you have the chance, go back in and open up your letter from God. Soak in His love for you. It'll do your heart good.

JEREMIAH 31:3 ESV

I have loved you with an everlasting love; therefore I have continued my faithfulness to you.

PRAYER

Your words are so beautiful. I don't have to wonder how You feel. You've written it on my heart, You've written it throughout creation, and You've written it in Your Love Letter. I cherish this eternal keepsake of Your devotion for me.

CELEBRATE EVERYTHING

DAY **69**

There is a small church in the South with the motto "Celebrate everything." I couldn't have said it better myself. I can imagine God agreeing too: "Yes, do it. Celebrate everything!"

He said as much when He instructed Old Testament Israel to gather seven times each year to commemorate His works and blessings with a major feast or festival. One look at the Bible's biggest book, the book of Psalms—which devotes entire chapters to praise and rejoicing—tells us that our God is a celebrating God. When we celebrate, we take on His character.

I realize it's not economical to throw an actual party every week, but we can take author John Ortberg's advice and devote a specific day of the week to a mini-celebration: a home-cooked meal with a friend, an outdoor hike, enjoying a movie that makes you laugh from the gut, attending an open-mic night at a coffeehouse, going for a swim. Anything that lifts your heart toward heaven and puts a smile on your face is a "God gift" worth acknowledging in some special way.[12]

All right, then! No more waiting for the big events. The everyday blessings deserve commemorating too.

PSALM 89:15–16

Blessed are those who have learned to acclaim you, who walk in the light of your presence, Lord. They rejoice in your name all day long; they celebrate your righteousness.

PRAYER

You give us so many reasons to celebrate! Let's pick a day this week, God, and do something special.

A PRETTY GOOD PERSON

DAY 70

After accepting Christ in my teens, very little about my life changed. I didn't think it needed to, because I was a moral person raised with great values, and I wasn't caught up in the stuff that a lot of other former child stars were involved in. Not until several years later, once the gospel message was presented to me in a way that held my goodness up against God's holiness, did I see the immense canyon between my standards and His.

An analogy that I love mentions a little girl who is watching a sheep eat grass in a field. The girl is amazed at how white the sheep looks in the middle of that dark-green pasture. Soon it begins to snow. The more it snows, the more she can see: That little sheep isn't so white after all. Against a pristine background, its grime was apparent.

As long as I compared my sin to the standard of the world, I was coming up reasonably clean. But upon comparing my sin to the perfection of Christ, I was confronted with how dirty my sins were. Even bigger for me, I newly understood that I had nothing to bring to God. All my efforts to establish my own righteousness were useless (Romans 10:3). My good works were "like filthy rags" (Isaiah 64:6). Essentially, I was as guilty as a criminal.

Being a pretty good person could never be good enough. I was wholesome but not whole. I needed Jesus to pay my debt and wash me in His righteousness.

It's out of gratitude for His saving grace that I want to live a life that serves and pleases Him. Our good works don't save us. They can't. Only God's grace, by faith in Christ alone. Praise God, that is enough!

ISAIAH 1:18

*"Come now, let us settle the matter," says the L*ORD*. "Though your sins are like scarlet, they shall be as white as snow; though they are red as crimson, they shall be like wool."*

PRAYER

Dearest Jesus, I can never adequately thank You for paying for my sins with Your own blood. I receive that undeserved gift and commit today to live wholeheartedly for You.

GREENHOUSE EFFECT

DAY 71

How quickly can you recall those situations that made your world smaller? You left your friends, your favorite coffee shop, and that home you renovated to move to a new town. An injury kept you homebound for weeks on end. A loved one got sick, and you became their primary caregiver. Or you gave up your full-time job to raise your kids.

Despite the passage of time, I remember those life-narrowing experiences like they were last week. No doubt you do too. How could we not? Making the transition from big world to small world will challenge anyone's identity, confidence, and sense of purpose—sometimes all on the same day!

What I didn't expect of those uncomfortable seasons, however, was to gain something so priceless and permanent. I gained a genuine friendship with God that is still growing strong.

I've said in the past that the ten years I was home raising my kids were like a greenhouse helping me grow. In that very specialized environment, my roots in Christ had a chance to deepen. The branches of my faith multiplied as I found out I could trust Him in ways I'd never known. And my love for Him blossomed, bearing even greater fruit after I was back in the wide world.

By using that time to tend to my friendship with God, I found that having a small world is a blessing after all. I pray that you'll discover this and more in your next growing season.

COLOSSIANS 1:9

We continually ask God to fill you with the knowledge of his will through all the wisdom and understanding that the Spirit gives.

PRAYER

How I long to know You better! Help me to worry less about the season I'm in and focus on my relationship with You.

SHRINKING WORRIES

DAY 72

A popular credit card company is currently running an ad campaign that ends with the question "What's in your wallet?" And, in a fun twist, a popular entertainment magazine does a photo shoot each issue of the contents of a celebrity's purse to let us see what the stars carry with them.

If God came calling today, not to feature what's in your wallet, or purse, but more importantly, to feature what's occupying your mind, would He find it jammed with "What if?" scenarios and worries about your needs? Or would He see evidence that you're entrusting your needs to Him?

The world pushes us to seek peace the same way it does: by trusting in our own strength, our own capacity to provide. Has self-sufficiency ever really quieted your mind, though? Nope? Me neither. Looking to ourselves piles on the stress and depletes our peace. Trusting our loving Father to look out for us is an entirely different outcome. The more we magnify Him, setting our minds on Him as our Source for all things, the smaller our worries become.

LUKE 12:22, 30–31 NLT

I tell you not to worry about everyday life—whether you have enough food to eat or enough clothes to wear. . . . These things dominate the thoughts of unbelievers all over the world, but your Father already knows your needs. Seek the Kingdom of God above all else, and he will give you everything you need.

PRAYER

I'm willing to open my wallet and my life to You, Father God, for You to do as You wish. In that scary step of faith, do Your work: Provide for me. Free me of my worries. Fill my mind to overflowing with Your peace.

STAY IN YOUR LANE

DAY 73

Of the many things Jesus modeled for us, I've probably looked to His example of gracious self-restraint the most. No way have I perfected it, but have I drawn on His treatment toward His enemies when I've been mocked or demeaned? Absolutely. Sometimes daily.

Jesus helps us control our fears about the way we're perceived, not just our temptation to fight back. He had a profound ability to "stay in His lane" and endure opposition. Beyond enduring, He left revenge in God's hands. This amazes me all the time because people can be cruel, and I know how terribly hard it is to trust God and not retaliate.

Jesus' way with His enemies is something we can replicate in the power of His Spirit. Jesus doesn't ask us to be silent before our accusers (in most situations) just as an exercise in godliness. He says we will be blessed for putting our opponents and our vindication in God's hands. Peace of mind will be ours. We won't burn any bridges that we might someday regret having burned. The Lord Himself will hear our cries for help and fight for us. And others will see Him through our response.

Today, should you need some extra incentive to stay in your lane and trust, take God's words to heart, right down to blessing those who curse you. His own Son has been exactly where we find ourselves right now, and He knows the surest route to peace. Peace with Him most of all.

Love your enemies, and pray for those who persecute you.
(Matthew 5:44 GW)

Do not repay evil with evil. . . . Whoever would love life and see good days must keep their tongue from evil. (1 Peter 3:9–10)

HEBREWS 12:3

Consider [Christ] who endured such opposition from sinners, so that you will not grow weary and lose heart.

PRAYER

Where I can be a peacemaker today, God, empower me. Instead of bitterness, fill my mouth with Your grace and my heart with Your forgiveness.

SURROUNDED

DAY **74**

What would we be like if you and I, assured of our identity as daughters of God, were confident that He would clearly guide us in our callings? We could be even bolder, don't you think? Happily, this is the truth we live in! As He calls, He provides.

Over and over again in Scripture, we see God calling or commissioning people to His purposes by a variety of means. Sometimes they were given their unique life purpose, such as Abraham, who was told he would father a great and chosen people as countless as the sand. More often, the Lord's followers were commissioned to specific acts.

You could name several of the big ones right off: Noah, building the ark; Moses, leading the Israelites out of Egypt; Elijah, facing down the prophets of Baal. But there are also plenty of everyday instances, such as the widow whom the Lord commanded to supply Elijah with food, and Ananias's assignment to visit a specific house on a specific street in his city and lay hands on a former religious persecutor as part of Saul's/Paul's preparation for ministry.

Each time God called, He also equipped and favored His sons and daughters for their tasks. Though many times His appointees were being sent into hostile environments on unprecedented missions, He specifically provided. For example, the disciples were given the words they needed when they were standing before ruling kings and religious officials. And when Joshua took over the leadership of Israel upon Moses' death, Deuteronomy 34:9 says he was "filled with the spirit of wisdom. . . . So the Israelites listened to him and did what the LORD had commanded Moses."

When the Lord sends us out, He won't leave us empty-handed: "Okay, beloved, you go and make it happen." Never! He prepares us, and our path, and our partners, as well as the hearts of those He intends for us to minister to.

PSALM 139:5 THE VOICE

You have surrounded me on every side, behind me and before me, and You have placed Your hand gently on my shoulder.

PRAYER

God, I love that You not only meet with Your children but provide practically for us. As this day unfolds, I will walk in faith that You have gone ahead of me and prepared the way.

DISCONNECTED

DAY 75

I've known my best friend, Dilini, since we were teenagers. We met at school, but our friendship really kicked into gear once our parents met. It didn't hurt that we lived close to each other either.

She and I recently passed our twenty-five-year "friendversary," and I thank God for her every single day. Reflecting on our shared journey together brings to mind some of those old friends with whom I've lost touch. Friendships fall by the wayside for all kinds of reasons—graduation, work relocations, packed schedules, the changing seasons of our lives, and, sadly, misunderstandings or unhealed wounds.

Within the church, people "drop out" for similar reasons. I get worried when friends in the faith who were once enthusiastic about being with other Christians suddenly disconnect and stay away.

May I make a suggestion about our approach in those situations? Rather than judging our brothers and sisters or getting mad, let's reach out and love them. A lot of people disconnect and isolate not because they like the distance, but because they haven't learned a better response. Since we know isolation is never the answer, we can offer them what is: community and friendship.

We women are natural connectors; we're relational and caring. What an opportunity to use that to each other's advantage! Coming alongside our spiritual sisters and letting them vent their frustrations about the church, or their fears or disappointments toward God, is a real ministry. We may be the only ones who ever ask them about the experiences that have turned them off.

Just by our asking, something within them could change. Through our willingness to have those transparent conversations, they might be encouraged to try again. Reconnect. Regain what was lost. They're certainly worth the try.

EPHESIANS 4:2-3

Be completely humble and gentle; be patient, bearing with one another in love. Make every effort to keep the unity of the Spirit through the bond of peace.

PRAYER

I know I've missed opportunities to minister to some of my friends because I failed to push past my own feelings to see their hurt. You bless us, God, with Your willingness to be in the mess with us for as long as it takes. Help me to do likewise without growing weary or impatient.

HEART HEALTH

DAY 76

What God does in us when we come to faith could be compared to a heart transplant: He gives us a new heart. With that new lease on life usually comes a desire to build up that heart and keep it strong.

To ensure our success after such a lifesaving procedure, the Great Physician has prescribed a long-term plan for heart health that includes exercise, good nutrition, fresh air and sunshine, and a strong support team. The exercise of spiritual disciplines and routines. The daily bread of His Word. The fresh air of forgiveness and repentance. Lots of Sonlight. And friends, family, and spiritual teachers who will support and encourage us.

God's plan includes His personal guarantee. We can trust it because His directives have been field-tested in the lab of life, verified in eternity, and given heaven's seal of approval. They will never be replaced or recalled, and they can't be improved on.

There's one surefire way I know to live healthy and live strong. Stay on Doctor's orders. He knows best.

PSALM 119:92-93 NLT

If your instructions hadn't sustained me with joy, I would have died in my misery. I will never forget your commandments, for by them you give me life.

PRAYER

Thank You for my new heart and my new chance at life.
I look to You and Your plan to cultivate daily routines
that will nourish my heart and lead me to health.

HAPPY IN HIM

DAY 77

On a scale of 1 to 100, how happy are you in God? Can you echo Isaiah's words: "All that I am rejoices in my God"?

Unless you were able to answer "100 percent" to both questions (I can see the teacher in *Ferris Bueller's Day Off* right now: "Anyone? Anyone?"), Pastor Matt Chandler suggests answering two other questions for ourselves that could move us further along in the right direction: "*What stirs your affection for Jesus Christ?* and *What robs you of those affections?*"[13]

In case it's hard to wrap your mind around those questions, think of your affections as hungers. What deepens your hunger for Jesus, and what shuts down your hunger for Him? Invite Jesus to work with you to figure out what is uniquely true of you.

No pleasure is too simple or small. A good run with your dog is just as legitimate as hugging your kid or cooking the perfect egg to start your day. If you're curious, my "stirrer list" includes hiking, being in nature, gardening, counting my blessings, time with family and friends, work, and avocado toast . . . while my robber list includes too much work and no rest, lack of exercise, fear, and loneliness. You might want to write or type your list and keep it handy. That way you can add to it as the Lord increases your hunger for Him.

ISAIAH 61:10 NCV

*The L*ORD *makes me very happy; all that I am rejoices in my God.*

PRAYER

Lord, prompt me to come to You as soon as I notice unhealthy patterns or start to chase fleeting satisfactions. Bring me back to my heart for You with renewed passion.

SEE THE UNSEEN

DAY 78

Every once in a while it hits me: *That same cashier has checked me out before, but I still don't know her name.* Or, *I spent twenty minutes in the taxi, and I never asked anything about the driver.* I'm a little embarrassed to admit that, in spite of knowing I'm not alone.

It's not what we intend. We don't mean to overlook or see past those strangers who quietly serve us each day. We just get in such a hurry that it happens by default.

Nevertheless, this is something I'd like to fix, starting now. Take my eyes off myself long enough to look some of these public servants in the eye, ask their name, and bless their work, their smile, their positive attitude. It only takes a few seconds, but what might those few seconds do for their spirits? What might it mean for them to be noticed and acknowledged?

They're there: behind the sandwich counter, pouring our coffee, lifting our luggage, giving us rides, manning the cash registers. Nameless to most people, but not to God. Unseen and unappreciated by the masses, but known intimately and adored by Him.

Maybe if you and I begin to look at them as He does, they'll realize He sees them too.

PSALM 138:6

Though the Lord is exalted, he looks kindly on the lowly; though lofty, he sees them from afar.

PRAYER

Lord, lessen my worries about myself so that my attention toward others may increase. I pray for more awareness to see the souls and meet the needs around me, whether it be a kind word, a listening ear, or a compliment.

DAY 79

REPRESENT!

Every person of faith is an ambassador for the kingdom of God, appointed by heaven's Commander in Chief to be His hands and voice to a hurting, needy world. By that privilege alone, you and I each have a platform from which God empowers us to bear witness to Him every day, for His glory.

You know me well enough by now to understand how real this calling is to me. I'm not sure a day goes by where I'm not evaluating some decision, some choice of mine, some words I've said, asking myself: "What will people say about Jesus because of me? What will they think of Him because of me?"

These are loaded questions, to be sure, but ones that are at the heart of why we have each been put on this earth, in this time and place, with the people we're among.

Today, be conscious of who you're serving, but don't be afraid either. Make God proud! Go out there and represent!

1 PETER 2:9–10 MSG

You are the ones chosen by God, chosen for the high calling of priestly work, chosen to be a holy people, God's instruments to do his work and speak out for him, to tell others of the night-and-day difference he made for you—from nothing to something, from rejected to accepted.

PRAYER

Lord, I so desire to represent You well to those who know You and to those who have yet to say yes to You. Instead of wanting to be right, persuade me to choose love. Develop in me the readiness to draw others to a deeper relationship with You.

YOUR FIRST AND BEST

DAY 80

Depending on our religious upbringing, or possibly our lack of one, we can easily confuse the ways of people with the ways of God. If I've been rejected by judgmental people, I might naturally assume that God is quick to condemn me as well. If a friend won't forgive me, maybe God can't forgive me either.

Probably every one of us can relate to this kind of thinking.

Our saving grace is that God's thoughts and ways are so much higher than ours. He is all-knowing, seeing every detail of every wound we've ever received. He knows what others have done to us; He has mercy where people don't. Also, He is all-loving, with compassion and grace to meet our every need. So a verse like this, which talks about pleasing God, need not scare or overwhelm us.

Pleasing God isn't like people-pleasing. When we people-please, we turn off a part of ourselves in order to, typically, keep the peace. With God, the motivation is love, not fear. Relationship over works. We bring our whole self to Him freely, knowing our position with Him is secure. We are His children, and nothing can ever change that. We can never lose His love—and we cannot earn it either.

To please God in the sense of Romans 12:1 involves offering ourselves as Christ did: voluntarily, wholly, out of overflowing love, not obligation. Very practically, it means giving God our first and best affections, energies, and gifts instead of the leftovers.

Once I understood what Jesus saved me from, I felt sincere gratitude, and that only deepens as the years pass. He has been so merciful to love us and cover our sins before any of us ever loved or even knew Him. I want to spend the rest of my life pleasing Him and trying to give Him my first and best! I feel His pleasure when I live this way. And His pleasure makes my heart sing.

Because God is who He is, you and I can feel free to please Him all day, every day! His pleasure is our pleasure.

ROMANS 12:1 GNT

So then, my friends, because of God's great mercy to us I appeal to you: Offer yourselves as a living sacrifice to God, dedicated to his service and pleasing to him. This is the true worship that you should offer.

PRAYER

I love that I can be my true self in Your presence. Where I've been holding back in fear, free me to revel in pleasing You.

BEYOND SKIN-DEEP

DAY 81

It's easy to read a passage like 1 Peter 3 from our modern perspective and think that the apostle was forbidding all the things we women do to look and feel good. But in the biblical context, Peter wasn't prohibiting nice accessories and clothes. Instead, he placed emphasis on what never goes out of style: the beauty of a gentle and quiet spirit. The message is that a soft, patient approach in a godly woman is far more likely to attract nonbelievers to Jesus (especially an unbelieving husband) than soft hair and skin.

We women don't need a lot of words to be persuasive. Our greatest allure is an irresistible inner beauty blessed by God that makes Jesus irresistible to others.

1 PETER 3:3-4

Your beauty should not come from outward adornment, such as elaborate hairstyles and the wearing of gold jewelry or fine clothes. Rather, it should be that of your inner self, the unfading beauty of a gentle and quiet spirit, which is of great worth in God's sight.

PRAYER

God, would You bless me with the kind of beauty that never fades? Quiet my spirit, tone down my tongue, perform the inner touch-ups I need to better attract people to You.

HE SEES YOU

DAY 82

I've been blessed to have a lot of good men in my life, including my dad; my big brother, Kirk; my husband, Val; and the guys from my second family: my TV dad, Bob Saget, and America's favorite uncles, Joey and Jesse (Dave Coulier and John Stamos).

You don't have to be around people like them for very long before their intent to help shines through. If somebody's angry, they try to calm them. If someone has been treated unjustly, they like to make it right. If something is broken, they want to fix it.

There are some situations, though, where I don't need a "fix" for a problem as much as I need my fears acknowledged. While in New York several years ago during my time on *The View*, I received word of a mass shooting back home in Southern California just before we went live on air. I was able to reach my son Lev and my husband and confirm that our three kids and their schools were safe. Still, I was undone at the thought of my worst nightmare as a mother.

That day, my cohost Whoopi Goldberg didn't poke her head in my dressing room and say, "Hey, the kids are fine, Candace. C'mon, breathe it out. Get some water and pull yourself together." No, she came quietly to my rescue in my dressing room, opened up her arms, and held me while I bawled my eyes out, saying little more than, "I've got you. I won't let you fall out there today. Just speak from your heart."

I won't forget that. Ever. She saw me, terror and tears combined, and was with me in it. And her actions told me so.

Physicians have been known to summarize the teaching of Hippocrates in saying, "You cannot always cure, but you can always comfort."[14] We have a God who is as mighty to save as He is to comfort. But for us women especially, we often need to see ahead of the solution.

The God who convinced a desperate mother that He saw her in her wilderness (Genesis 16:1–16) sees our brokenness. Our rawness. Our fear. He comes to our rescue, yes. He hears and responds to our cries for help, absolutely. But He never, ever forgets our need for that tender, face-to-face connection that says, "I see you, and I'm with you."

GENESIS 16:13

[Hagar] gave this name to the Lord who spoke to her: "You are the God who sees me," for she said, "I have now seen the One who sees me."

PRAYER

Don't forget about me, God. Come to my rescue. I'll know You're with me as soon as I can look You in the eyes and see that You see me.

GROW TOWARD THE LIGHT

DAY 83

From the pages of Proverbs, wisdom beckons to us: "Absorb God's truth. Don't turn away. Open up and take it in." As much as flowers need sunlight for their growth, we need the focused truth of God's Word for ours. Every bit as much. It's sunshine to our souls, like when a plant is positioned properly in a windowsill.

Anyone who doesn't bother to open their Bible misses it all, including the boost of spiritual nutrients that accompanies exposure to the light of God's Word.

While we absorb the principles, promises, commands, and priorities of Scripture, the Holy Spirit illuminates our hearts and minds, converting those words into good works and love for others. By this divine form of photosynthesis, we grow more lovely and loving, more sturdy and strong over time.

Not only is the Word of God health and life to our bones, but it fortifies us for life "outdoors," in the real world. Philippians 2:14–16 says that by conducting ourselves as children of God, we will "go out into the world uncorrupted, a breath of fresh air in this squalid and polluted society," providing people with "a glimpse of good living and of the living God" (MSG).

The more of God and His Word that we take in, the more of God and His love we will be able to breathe out. Photosynthesis is a beautiful thing.

PROVERBS 4:20-22 NLT

My child, pay attention to what I say. Listen carefully to my words. Don't lose sight of them. Let them penetrate deep into your heart, for they bring life to those who find them, and healing to their whole body.

PRAYER

Your words breathe life into my being.
Grant me a fresh love of Your Word.

FROM THE HEART

DAY 84

As much as I love to give gifts, I also enjoy receiving them. Among the most memorable things I've ever received was a peridot and diamond cocktail ring, given to me by Val for my twenty-first birthday. It's still my most special and favorite piece of jewelry to date.

We would probably all agree that the best gifts have one thing in common: They come from the heart. George MacDonald wrote, "For the real good of every gift, it is essential that the giver be in the gift—as God always is, for he is love—and, next, that the receiver know and receive the giver in the gift. Every gift of God is but a harbinger of his greatest and only sufficing gift—that of himself."[15]

What ways can you give of yourself today? This kind of generosity isn't about the expense involved. Who needs your smile to warm up their day? Who needs your kindness to ease their distress? Who needs to know you're thinking of them, that you believe in them, that you're grateful for them, that you cherish them and the memories you've made together?

A text, an email, a little card, a phone call—any of these things can be your gift from the heart today, sealed with a kiss from heaven.

ROMANS 8:32

He who did not spare his own Son, but gave him up for us all—how will he not also, along with him, graciously give us all things?

PRAYER

Just as You give from the heart, Jesus, I want to do the same. I pray You'll show me who to bless and by what means I can bless them best.

UNSHAKEN

DAY 85

Because I live in earthquake-prone California, the unshakable nature of Christ and His eternal kingdom is tangible to me. To know that as long as I'm grounded in Him, my faith cannot be brought down or destroyed, regardless of the news I hear and no matter what others do—what a difference that makes!

The prophet reminded King Hezekiah in Isaiah 33:6 that the Lord "will be the sure foundation for your times, a rich store of salvation and wisdom and knowledge." Jesus is the solid rock from which we operate in the world. He is the base from which we launch and the strength on which we stand firm.

The Bible promises that those who build their lives on Him will never be put to shame (Romans 10:11). Not only that, but as God's people, we have received an entire kingdom that cannot be shaken (Hebrews 12:28-29)! We worship the One who is called faithful and true in the book of Revelation (19:11). Neither His Word nor His character will ever change (Malachi 3:6). With Jesus as our sure foundation, we will not be moved (Isaiah 33:6). Stand strong with me in this today.

PSALM 18:1-2 ESV

I love you, O LORD, my strength. The LORD is my rock and my fortress and my deliverer, my God, my rock, in whom I take refuge, my shield . . . my stronghold.

PRAYER

God, You hold me steady when waves of chaos or uncertainty crash over me. I look to You to keep me standing no matter what comes my way.

LIFELINE

DAY 86

Ever since my parents started taking us to church when I was twelve, I've liked it. I also liked what it did for my family. Gathering consistently with a community of believers not only saved my parents' marriage but introduced all four of us kids to a lifelong relationship with Christ.

It was a lifeline then, and it's been a lifeline for my own family since Val and I were married. Particularly in some of the more trying seasons of my life, I've leaned on my brothers and sisters in the faith for prayer and accountability and support. The music and positive messages have also offered me a much-needed reset before heading back out into the world.

To come together with other believers as often as we can is invaluable. As we fellowship and worship and are strengthened by the truths of God's Word, joining with the family of God allows us to return our sights to Christ so that we may, in turn, exit our houses of worship and take His light into our neighborhoods and homes and workplaces.

Whether you're needing a little pick-me-up or could really use a lifeline for holding fast to your faith, seek out a local group of believers with whom you can do life. And if you've been deeply wounded by a church or its spiritual leaders in the past, can I encourage you to try again? For a time in my early adult years, I wasn't such a regular myself, but once I started going back, I could see what I'd been missing.

It may take a while to find your faith tribe, but they're out there. God's family comes in all shapes and sizes these days, and they meet in movie theaters and coffeehouses and barns, even online, not just in steepled buildings. Give His people a chance, and see what God may have in store for you.

HEBREWS 10:24-25

Let us consider how we may spur one another on toward love and good deeds, not giving up meeting together, as some are in the habit of doing, but encouraging one another—and all the more as you see the Day approaching.

PRAYER

Would You lead me to a faith community where I fit in and where I can grow? I pray for patience and an extra measure of discernment while I search.

TRIAL BY FIRE

DAY **87**

This story in Daniel 3 is a children's church favorite and, truth be told, maybe a favorite in big people's church too: that of the three young men—Shadrach, Meshach, and Abednego—whom God delivered from King Nebuchadnezzar's blazing furnace.

Those Hebrew teenagers had served the king of Babylon with excellence, except that they wouldn't worship his newly built statue. That statue was covered in gold and stood ninety feet tall and nine feet wide, a symbol of Babylon's power as well as the king's. It was massive enough to block out the sun if somebody stood in the right spot.

Threatened with fire if they didn't fall down and worship the idol, Shadrach, Meshach, and Abednego were backed into a corner: Compromise or stay true to the God they served. "King Nebuchadnezzar," they responded, "we do not need to defend ourselves before you in this matter. If we are thrown into the blazing furnace, the God we serve is able to deliver us from it.... But even if he does not, we want you to know, Your Majesty, that we will not serve your gods or worship the image of gold you have set up" (vv. 16–18).

You know the rest of the story. The three friends were tied up, thrown in the inferno, and ... nothing happened, except that they were joined supernaturally by a fourth figure, whom the king said looked like "a son of the gods" (v. 25). Not a hair on their heads was singed, and they didn't even smell like smoke. This convinced the king that these young men were more than servants in his kingdom; they were servants of the Most High God.

What corner have you been backed into? Who is trying to block your view of the Son? Are you being badgered to "calm down" or "lighten up" about your morals and be part of the crowd? Is someone suggesting that you turn your back on God because He's not going to save you? Say with Job, and the psalmists, and Daniel, and Daniel's three friends, and so many people of faith past and present: "No matter what comes, I will trust in Him" (see Job 13:15).

Trials by fire are no joke. When we take a stand of loyalty, we never know what lies ahead. We may see a good result with unbelieving hearts turned to the Lord. Other times, we may be oppressed or rejected for our faith. Yet God promises this: We can cast aside our fear, for we belong to Him. When we pass through the fire, He will be right there with us.

2 CHRONICLES 16:9 NKJV

The eyes of the Lord run to and fro throughout the whole earth, to show himself strong on behalf of those whose heart is loyal to him.

PRAYER

You are my Defender and Deliverer. Whether I'm being cornered by someone close to me or someone in authority, I trust that You will vindicate the faith I have in You.

MAKE UP YOUR MIND

DAY 88

Whoever said "Old habits die hard" wasn't kidding! It'd be pretty easy to toss in the towel and just keep doing what we've always done—except that Christ has made a way to leave those old habits behind once and for all. He does this by renewing our minds. It's part of the gift of the gospel, given to us at our spiritual birth.

This renewed mind is actually the mind of Christ at work within us, orienting us toward God's desires so that our choices can align with His. Every time they do, God is pleased. So are we. His wisdom infuses our lives with joy.

Taking a cue from Joshua during his days as Israel's leader, planning ahead is a good use of our transformed mind. It's one of God's best weapons for fighting temptation and the tug of old thinking.

"Choose this day whom you will serve," Joshua declared. "As for me and my house, we will serve the LORD" (Joshua 24:15 ESV). He was all about defining values, loyalties, and priorities in advance. This has helped me immensely as a wife, mom, and career woman. Realizing that I could preempt temptation and determine my boundary lines ahead of the hot seat was huge. For Val and me to establish our nonnegotiables as a couple before they were tested has further united us as parents and fortified our marriage.

Like anybody, compromise has come looking for me and my family more than once. Criticism and peer pressure have come our way many, many times. But the bedrock decisions have already been made. We're able to remain strong because we have the mind of Christ, and He is the Rock on which we stand.

EPHESIANS 5:16 GNT

Make good use of every opportunity you have, because these are evil days.

PRAYER

Thank You, Lord, that You take such great care of my daily life. Because You have been my strength in times of temptation, I trust you will guide me to new ways of thinking.

FIRST RESPONDERS

DAY 89

I'm so thankful for the first responders in our communities—those men and women who have such a heart for others that they've trained to be able to administer help in someone's hour of need.

By virtue of our relationship with Christ, we have been spiritually equipped as first responders in others' times of need. Not only do we have the heart for it thanks to Jesus' sacrifice for us, but we have His Spirit, the divine Helper, prompting us toward the needs that surround us and training us to come alongside those who are weak, grieving, hurt, or afraid.

Others may walk on by the need right in front of them, but we won't. God has readied us for service. We're in position to lend a hand—and to do so without thinking twice—all because we have been sent out by Christ Himself.

JAMES 2:15–17 ESV

If a brother or sister is poorly clothed and lacking in daily food, and one of you says to them, "Go in peace, be warmed and filled," without giving them the things needed for the body, what good is that? So also faith by itself, if it does not have works, is dead.

PRAYER

Jesus, You've been my rescue in every time of need. Equip me today to see the needs around me and to be quick to respond to them.

OPEN HANDS, OPEN HEART

DAY 90

When Jesus told His disciples that their heart would be wherever their treasure was, He was urging them to pursue God and His kingdom priorities beyond anything else. His kingdom is powered by love—God's love for us, our love for Him, and our love for one another because of Christ's love for us—and known for its joy.

Jesus wanted His followers to uphold different standards so that God's kingdom could come and His will be done on earth as it is in heaven. Give instead of get. Trust instead of worry. Bless instead of withhold. Value love over money.

Having nice things has never been God's issue. He delights in blessing us, and He lavishes us with so many gifts each day that we can't count them. He just doesn't want the blessing to stop there. Neither does He want us treating anything with a short shelf life as valuable. He commands us to avoid attachments to what doesn't last. His message is "Hold everything of this earth loosely."

A great way to encourage such open hands is to give, frequently and generously.

Two ideas come to mind. First, give up something each week. For years, our family has opted to each individually forgo a small something, such as the purchase of a cup of coffee on Wednesdays or a toy when the kids were younger, and donate that money instead to someone who needs it. Second, let receiving prompt your giving. Every time an unexpected gift or a "goodness" (a paycheck, a favor, any kind of help) comes your way—find someone to whom you can forward a little of that joy.

To both give and receive a gift, we must open our hands. Our generous God has designed it to work that way. He loves to see His children open their hands to receive with gratitude and open their hands to lavish love on others.

Open hands, open heart, adding joy upon joy. That's heaven's way. Let's make it ours as well.

MATTHEW 6:21 NCV

Your heart will be where your treasure is.

PRAYER

Lord, all that I have is Yours. So why is it so difficult for me to get past the momentary pleasure of a possession? Move in my heart to hold things loosely so I can freely receive all that You have for me and then offer Your gifts to others.

HOW OLD ARE YOU?

DAY 91

Adulting is not easy! Finding a place to live, being responsible for your bills and credit score, keeping steady employment, or overseeing a house and kids—those logistical challenges are biggies. Maybe tougher, though, is something that rarely gets mentioned: attaining emotional and spiritual maturity. Our mentors or pastors or parents may speak to this, but almost no one else does.

Except God. He cares about this a lot. Judging by the hundreds of Bible verses involving these themes, our maturity matters significantly more to Him than how well we organize our lives; though as a God of order, He'd probably say an organized life is also worth shooting for.

Looking back at my own childhood and adolescence, I can think of two characteristics that broadcasted to the adults around me that I was still a kid. Being driven by my emotions was one. *I want that. Now! . . . It's your fault, not mine! . . . You can't make me! . . . You hate me! I just know it!* Who among us didn't say or at least feel those exact things back in the day? The other characteristic was being susceptible to peer pressure. We know this starts when we're little, but it picks up momentum in our teens.

I'd compare trusting our feelings to letting a three-year-old run the household of our heart. Can you imagine? Likewise, trusting our friends' opinions or culture's standards over God's is the equivalent of running with the bulls in Pamplona. Both are accidents waiting to happen, and thus, no way for us to live.

Little kids follow their emotions; teenagers follow the crowd. Not adults.

Knowing that we are made for maturity, do a little self-evaluation every once in a while to ask: *How old am I emotionally? Spiritually?* With God's grace and guidance, that number will surely increase with time. I look forward to it! It's one instance where I have zero qualms about growing old!

---

1 CORINTHIANS 13:11 NCV

When I was a child, I talked like a child, I thought like a child, I reasoned like a child. When I became a man, I stopped those childish ways.

PRAYER

Lord, I'm not proud of my fits and temper tantrums or my "do as the world does" attitudes. I need Your help to be able to accomplish all that You have planned for me. Set my sights on You, Jesus, and Your example of maturity in heart, mind, and spirit.

STRONG ARMS

DAY 92

Reading today's verse, I picture this proverbial woman of God as being in the afterglow of a good workout, focusing on her triceps and biceps and getting all dressed up for a great night out. Okay, okay, so maybe that's not the exact scenario, but she obviously cares about dressing well and being strong.

Personally, I'm relieved that God commends this, aren't you? Tending to those two aspects of life produces more confidence and poise, and when we feel our best, we're more likely to give others our best.

It all makes sense to me on a physical level, but I was curious: What does this mean spiritually? Some Bible translations refer to this virtuous woman as girding herself with strength, as if she were cinching a belt around the core of her body. In other words, she is preparing her entire self—body, mind, emotions, and spirit—for action.

What do you do to strengthen yourself to go out and face the world? Eating well, exercising, getting good sleep, and studying God's Word are all ways I make myself ready to do the work God has called me to. Prayer is another big one. It reminds me that I never go alone. Neither do you.

PROVERBS 31:17 ESV

She dresses herself with strength and makes her arms strong.

PRAYER

Lord God, would You prepare me for the action and activity of this day? I can do anything that You ask me to do, as long as You are the one making me strong.

WHENEVER I CALL YOU FRIEND

DAY 93

I'm always a little awestruck when I read in Exodus 33:11 that "the LORD would speak to Moses face to face, as one speaks to a friend" (NLT). I can't imagine what that must have been like. Moses was among the few people in Old Testament times who consistently heard from the Lord directly, and he was the only one who walked and talked with God in exactly that way.

Jesus' arrival on earth signaled a new era. As soon as He finished His work on the cross, no longer would the people of God access Him through human agents such as priests or prophets. Forever after, His disciples in any era would be able to approach Him directly with their thoughts and requests, worries and fears.

That title, "friend," is among the most beautiful titles on earth. Through it, Jesus was giving believers an all-access pass to His life and heart along with that of His Father.

Do you speak to Him as you would a beloved friend? Or are you keeping Him at arm's length, as we often do a boss or authority figure? Jesus reached out in friendship first. That says so much to me! We can leave our fears of intimacy behind and really open up to Him, seeking Him out when we're troubled, running to Him when we're sad, trusting Him always.

You have a Friend who is on call all day long, eager to talk or listen. Reach out whenever you need to or whenever you just feel like talking. He loves hearing your voice and your heart.

JOHN 15:15

I no longer call you servants. . . . Instead, I have called you friends, for everything that I learned from my Father I have made known to you.

PRAYER

What a faithful friend You are, God! I'm blessed by Your friendship, which is so pure and good. I never have to wonder if I can count on You. May You be able to say the same of me.

TEN TIMES BETTER

DAY 94

As a Christian, are you known for your excellent efforts? I intentionally didn't ask about your success but about your striving for excellence. After nearly three decades in show business, I'm more aware than ever of how little I control the results of my efforts; only the quality of effort is in my hands.

To type As, that might sound like a downer, until you consider this upside: Whether our efforts succeed or fail leaves less of an impression on others than our work ethic. Good companies and teams and causes still want people who show up every day and put in a full day. Hard work outshines lazy talent any day. In business and everywhere else, trust is the highest commodity. It has to be earned. And it is a success in its own right. As we prove faithful in small things, those in authority, including God, entrust us with bigger things.

Of the dozens of Bible verses that endorse godly effort, the most telling passages might be the accounts of those who faithfully gave their best day in and day out. Joseph, before he became vice pharaoh of Egypt, proved faithful as chief of staff of an Egyptian official's entire household. The man entrusted everything he owned to Joseph's care, we're told. "With Joseph in charge, [Potiphar] did not concern himself with anything except the food he ate" (Genesis 39:6). As far as Daniel and his friends . . . when they were presented by their supervisor, the chief official, to the king of Babylon to enter his service, the king "found none equal" to them. According to the biblical account, "in every matter of wisdom and understanding about which the king questioned them, he found them ten times better" than all the advisers in the land (Daniel 1:19–20).

In everything you're given to do, carry out your responsibilities with excellence. Show up on time or a little early. Do your homework so you're ready and able to give your best. And treat others right. Your peers might not like it; they may claim you're a show-off. So what? Stay humble and stay at it. Work harder and apply yourself better than anyone else does. You know the truth: You're not doing it to get ahead (although that will likely happen naturally); you're doing it for the ones you serve and the One you love most of all.

---

2 CORINTHIANS 9:8, 10 NASB

God is able to make all grace overflow to you, so that, always having all sufficiency in everything, you may have an abundance for every good deed. . . . He who supplies seed to the sower and bread for food will supply and multiply your seed for sowing and increase the harvest of your righteousness.

PRAYER

I want to be faithful in little so I can be faithful in much. God, thank You for a renewed focus and renewed strength so I can be a good steward in this season I'm in.

POINT OF CONTACT

DAY 95

I wish it wasn't true, but in our culture especially, people will judge an entire product line or company based on one point of contact. A single sales or customer-service experience can be the difference between lifelong loyalty or a lifetime of negative reviews.

Things operate much the same way when people walk into a church for the first time and when they meet us (whether inside the church or out in the world). Obviously, our faith isn't a product line and Jesus isn't a brand, yet the principle applies for every one of us who claims to follow Him: We may be the only "Jesus" some people will ever meet. Their opinions and future openness to Him could be shaped by how we treat these potential Christians from the first hello. Handle them with care, lots of love, and maybe a little humor too. They might be family one day.

2 CORINTHIANS 2:14-15 ESV

Thanks be to God, who . . . through us spreads the fragrance of the knowledge of [Christ] everywhere. For we are the aroma of Christ to God among those who are being saved and among those who are perishing.

PRAYER

Lord, no matter what I'm going through personally, I pray that Your Holy Spirit will shine through me and touch the people I meet with a beautiful glimpse of You.

WILLPOWER

DAY 96

Every Christian receives both a new heart and a new spirit upon being born again. For those who understand the miracle of God's work, obvious changes take place almost immediately. Where we used to live to please ourselves, we begin to want what pleases the Lord. Our past desires lose some of their hold, and God increasingly empowers us to do His will. In the truest sense of the word, we gain a double portion of willpower as never before.

Sadly, some believers—for reasons I can't entirely explain—don't ever seem to develop that extra layer of strength. Instead of growing "strong-willed" in the Lord (which is the only kind of strong will we want), they remain weak-willed. Maybe they simply haven't been taught that God, through the Holy Spirit, has more power on reserve, available at any time.

Have you asked the Holy Spirit for more of His power lately? You can, you know. Are you working out your spiritual muscles to further develop your strength? We ought to be. It will only supplement what Christ is already doing.

Our Training Partner promises to stay in it with us until we've accomplished the goal. So push through your spiritual workouts, and don't let up. He is making all things strong and new, including you and your will!

PHILIPPIANS 2:13 NLT

God is working in you, giving you the desire and the power to do what pleases him.

PRAYER

Salvation is just the beginning of a beautiful journey with You. I will use Your strength to continually cultivate my new heart and spirit in pursuit of a life that pleases You.

YOUR BEST DAY EVER

DAY 97

Did you watch Prince Harry and Meghan Markle's royal wedding? The better question might be: Did you catch the entire live broadcast or a few minutes of highlights afterward?

It seems like the entire world turns out for a British royal wedding. Our friends in London are masters at making a wedding a global event. The pageantry and uniforms, the music, the joyous bells of Westminster Abbey, the dresses and hats worn by notable guests—we don't see anything else like it anywhere, except for what we read of heaven, that is.

"Joy is the serious business of heaven," wrote C. S. Lewis.[16] Celebrations are crucial to our spiritual life because they anchor us in a deeper, wider story. We may currently be undergoing hardship and pain. Praise and feasting and happy reunions connect us to that future day when God's entire family from every corner of heaven and earth will come together for the wedding feast between the bride of Christ, His church (which is each and every person who has ever believed in Him as Savior), and the Bridegroom Himself, the King of kings and Lord of lords.

Consider the lavish wedding preparation for the biggest wedding event yet to come, hosted by the House of God, the Royals of Eternity. You've already been invited. Make sure you RSVP, and then start getting ready. It will literally be your best day ever!

REVELATION 19:7

Let us rejoice and be glad and give him glory! For the wedding of the Lamb has come, and his bride has made herself ready.

PRAYER

Thinking about the day You come back for Your people, Jesus, brings me such excitement and joy. Help me to be a person whose days are marked by joy, no matter my circumstances.

SHOUT-OUT

DAY 98

Some motivational speakers have said that, for most people, the last round of applause they ever received was at their high school graduation. There isn't one person in our offices, our schools, our neighborhoods, our churches, or even our own homes who doesn't crave a little recognition.

A little appreciation goes a long way. It's the number-one factor in workplace satisfaction, and it's a key to any close relationship.

Malini Bhatia, the founder and CEO of Marriage.com, will often suggest to couples that they start thanking their partners for every little thing they do. To skip this, she says, is "a sign that you think the bigger things you do (or believe you do) are not as important as the little things that your partner does."[17]

You can start making your list here, but also make a point to follow up. Shout out to God for His wondrous works and His unlimited love for you. Shout out to your loved ones for the daily things they do that express love or keep your household running. And give a shout-out to the people around you who are doing good every day. Pay special attention to the ones in your circle who are most likely to go unrecognized: men and women who live alone (whether single or divorced or widowed); the shy types; the ones behind the scenes who quietly stay at their task; those who are disadvantaged in some way; and those who do the work that people tend to describe as "blue collar" or "menial."

If any of those descriptors fits you, I applaud you today. God does too. He couldn't care less about collars, and no job is menial in His eyes. He appreciates what you do, day in and day out. I pray He will remind you of that somehow in this day.

PSALM 95:1-3 TPT

Come on, everyone! Let's sing for joy to the Lord! Let's shout our loudest praises to our God who saved us! Everyone come meet his face with a thankful heart. Don't hold back your praises. . . . For the Lord is the greatest of all, King-God over all other gods!

PRAYER

Lord, thank You that You see me, even when it feels like I'm invisible. I pray for a greater capacity to notice the efforts of others so I can express my gratitude to them.

REMEMBERED

DAY 99

How would you like to be remembered? Good interviewers often ask a question like this, but it's vital for each of us to answer it for ourselves.

I've occasionally heard people dismiss the topic, saying, "That's morbid. I don't want to think about dying." However, in my mind, this question is central to living our best and fullest life.

Rabbi Harold Kushner explained in an interview, "It's not mortality that frightens us, it's invisibility, the dreadful feeling that neither our living nor our dying will make a difference to the world."

Life is short, but we can make a long-lasting difference by living beyond ourselves. Faith and service are key—far more important than our bank account or reputation. "We may not be famous," said Rabbi Kushner, "but we matter to the people close to us, and we matter to God."[18] To make a difference, we have to build from there. Not everyone will be able to leave an inheritance, and very few of us will ever have a building with our name on it. Every one of us, however, can bequeath something to our successors. May our legacy be one of love, grace, and forgiveness and a testimony of lifelong trust in God.

ACTS 20:24

My only aim is to finish the race and complete the task the Lord Jesus has given me—the task of testifying to the good news of God's grace.

PRAYER

Lord, I want to leave a legacy that lasts for generations. I pray that out of a greater intimacy with You will spring forth a greater awareness of my purpose and how to practically carry that out.

TAKE HEART

DAY **100**

A 2014 study declared millennials, especially women, the most anxious generation of all. But it's not just millennials. Surveys by the American Psychiatric Association reveal that our national anxiety is increasing, from baby boomers to the teenagers of Generation Z. Today's sixteen-year-olds seem to have the anxiety levels of fifty-year-olds of the past.[19] Which means we are no longer a people who anticipate but a people riddled with worry.

I'm not an anxious person by nature, but my heart goes out to the many friends I know and meet who do consistently struggle with it. When I am feeling anxious, nothing soothes me as much as the balm of God's own words. So instead of trying to comfort you with my own reassurances, do you mind if I share a few of God's promises that calm my heart and mind?

*I wait for the LORD, my whole being waits, and in his word
I put my hope. (Psalm 130:5)*

We are pressed on every side by troubles, but we are not crushed. We are perplexed, but not driven to despair. We are hunted down, but never abandoned by God. We get knocked down, but we are not destroyed. (2 Corinthians 4:8–9 NLT)

As for me, I watch in hope for the LORD, I wait for God my Savior; my God will hear me. Do not gloat over me, my enemy! Though I have fallen, I will rise. Though I sit in darkness, the LORD will be my light. (Micah 7:7–8)

You are very, very loved.

PSALM 27:13-14

I remain confident of this: I will see the goodness of the LORD in the land of the living. Wait for the LORD; be strong and take heart and wait for the LORD.

PRAYER

Whatever you're going through today, my sisters, I'd like to pray for you as we close out our time together. In the name of Jesus, may you find deep blessing and assurance in the knowledge that He conquered the powers of darkness and dread so you wouldn't have to. I pray His strength, and joy, and abiding peace over you as you live for Him. And may He, the God of hope, "fill you with all joy and peace as you trust in him, so that you may overflow with hope by the power of the Holy Spirit" (Romans 15:13).

NOTES

1. Renée Onque, "An Act of Generosity Is One of the 'Quickest and Easiest Ways to Get Happier'—Here's Why," February 28, 2024, cnbc.com, https://www.cnbc.com/2024/02/28/heres-the-science-behind-why-you-feel-happier-after-being-generous.html.

2. Sam Levenson, *In One Era and Out the Other* (G. K. Hall, 1974).

3. Jackie Green and Lauren Green McAfee, *Only One Life* (Thomas Nelson, 2018).

4. Charles John Ellicott, *A New Testament Commentary for English Readers*, vol. 3 (Cassell and Company, 1897), 361.

5. "Brain Development," First Things First, accessed March 14, 2025, https://files.firstthingsfirst.org/for-parents-and-families/brain-development.

6. Claudia Hammond, "Prattle of the Sexes: Do Women Talk More Than Men?" BBC, November 11, 2013, https://www.bbc.com/future/article/20131112-do-women-talk-more-than-men.

7. Paul Petrone, "You Speak (at Least) 7,000 Words a Day. Here's How to Make Them Count," LinkedIn, August 17, 2017, https://www.linkedin.com/business/learning/blog/career-success-tips/you-speak-at-least-7-000-words-a-day-here-s-how-to-make-them.

8. Mel Schwartz, "Our Words Matter," *Psychology Today*, accessed March 14, 2025, https://www.psychologytoday.com/us/blog/a-shift-of-mind/201904/our-words-matter.

9. Charles Haddon Spurgeon, "The Profit of Godliness in the Life to Come," *Metropolitan Tabernacle Pulpit Volume 16* (1870), Spurgeon.org, accessed March 14, 2025, https://www.spurgeon.org/resource-library/sermons/the-profit-of-godliness-in-the-life-to-come/#flipbook/.

10. "O. S. Hawkins on Influence," posted March 13, 2024, by The Postscript, episode 187, YouTube.com, :04, https://www.youtube.com/watch?v =KM5ar6v3oBQ.

11. Nicole Johnson, *Dropping Your Rock* (Thomas Nelson, 2011).

12. John Ortberg, *The Life You've Always Wanted* (Zondervan, 2015).

13. Justin Taylor, "Chandler: Two Questions for Sanctification," *The Gospel Coalition*, September 9, 2009, https://www.thegospelcoalition.org/blogs/justin-taylor/chandler-two-questions-for/.

14. David J. Armstrong, "Cure Sometimes, Care Always," *Ulster Medical Journal* 93, no. 1 (2024): https://pmc.ncbi.nlm.nih.gov/articles/PMC11067305/.

15. George MacDonald, *Unspoken Sermons* (Sea Harp Press, 2022), 197.

16. C. S. Lewis, *Letters to Malcolm, Chiefly on Prayer* (HarperOne, 2017), chapter 17.

17. Malini Bhatia, "The Importance of Appreciation in a Relationship," HuffPost, September 4, 2017, https://www.huffpost.com/entry/the-importance-of-appreciation-in-a-relationship_b_59ad1b54e4b0d0c16bb52671.

18. "Harold Kushner Interview: The Power of Simple Things," IndieBound.org, accessed March 14, 2025, https://www.indiebound.org/author-interviews/kushnerharold.

19. Sophie Bethune, "Teen Stress Rivals That of Adults," *American Psychological Association* 45, no. 4 (April 2014), https://www.apa.org/monitor/2014/04/teen-stress.

For an exclusive video guide and extended scripture readings, experience
100 Days of Joy and Strength
with Candace at candace.com/together.

Candace Cameron Bure is an actress, producer, and *New York Times* bestselling author. She is beloved by millions worldwide as everyone's big sister, D.J. Tanner, from the iconic television shows *Full House* and *Fuller House*, has starred in more than 50 Christmas and cozy mystery movies, and is a former cohost of *The View*. She is CEO of CandyRock Entertainment and host of her self-titled podcast. Candace is both outspoken and passionate about her family and faith and continues to flourish in the entertainment industry as a role model to women of all ages.

www.candace.com

candacecbure

candacecameron

candacecameronb

BIBLE TRANSLATIONS USED

Scripture quotations marked AMPC are taken from the Amplified® Bible (AMPC). Copyright © 1954, 1958, 1962, 1964, 1965, 1987 by The Lockman Foundation. Used by permission. www.lockman.org.

Scripture quotations marked ESV are taken from the ESV® Bible (The Holy Bible, English Standard Version®). Copyright © 2001 by Crossway, a publishing ministry of Good News Publishers. All rights reserved.

Scripture quotations marked GNT are taken from the Good News Translation® in Today's English Version—Second Edition. Copyright © 1992 by American Bible Society. Used by permission.

Scripture quotations marked GW are taken from God's Word®. © 1995, 2003, 2013, 2014, 2019, 2020 by God's Word to the Nations Mission Society. Used by permission.

Scripture quotations marked HCSB are taken from the Holman Christian Standard Bible®, Copyright © 1999, 2000, 2002, 2003, 2009 by Holman Bible Publishers. Used by permission. Holman Christian Standard Bible®, Holman CSB®, and HCSB® are federally registered trademarks of Holman Bible Publishers.

Scripture quotations marked KJV are taken from the King James Version. Public domain.

Scripture quotations marked MSG are taken from *The Message*. Copyright © 1993, 2002, 2018 by Eugene H. Peterson. Used by permission of NavPress. All rights reserved. Represented by Tyndale House Publishers, Inc.

Scripture quotations marked NASB are taken from the (NASB®) New American Standard Bible®, Copyright © 1960, 1971, 1977, 1995, 2020 by The Lockman Foundation. Used by permission. All rights reserved. www.lockman.org.

Scripture quotations marked NCV are taken from the New Century Version®. Copyright © 2005 by Thomas Nelson. Used by permission. All rights reserved.

Scripture quotations marked NKJV are taken from the New King James Version®. Copyright © 1982 by Thomas Nelson. Used by permission. All rights reserved.

Scripture quotations marked NLT are taken from the Holy Bible, New Living Translation. Copyright © 1996, 2004, 2015 by Tyndale House Foundation. Used by permission of Tyndale House Publishers, Carol Stream, Illinois 60188. All rights reserved.

Scripture quotations marked TLB are taken from *The Living Bible*. Copyright © 1971 by Tyndale House Foundation. Used by permission of Tyndale House Publishers, Carol Stream, Illinois 60188. All rights reserved.

Scripture quotations marked TPT are taken from The Passion Translation®. Copyright © 2017, 2018, 2020 by Passion & Fire Ministries, Inc. Used by permission. All rights reserved. ThePassionTranslation.com.

Scripture quotations marked THE VOICE are taken from The Voice.™ Copyright © 2012 by Ecclesia Bible Society. Used by permission. All rights reserved.